Reckoning: Our Beautiful Reward
Electronic Edition: Fall 2022
Print Edition: Spring 2023

Reckoning *is a communal effort.*
Editorial staff, in alphabetical order:

Cover and text ornament by Mona Robles

Reckoning Press
206 East Flint Street
Lake Orion, MI 48362
www.reckoning.press
distributed by IngramSpark

 ISSN 2474-7327
e-ISBN 978-1-955360-06-7
print ISBN 978-1-955360-07-4

Reckoning:
Our Beautiful Reward

Contents

Editorial: Naming names, claiming days.

Catherine Rockwood

These are the Supreme Court Justices of the United States of America who voted to overturn Roe v. Wade on June 24, 2022.

John Roberts
Samuel Alito
Clarence Thomas
Neil Gorsuch
Amy Coney Barrett
Brett Kavanaugh

Five Justices had stated publicly in the past—sometimes the very recent past—that they regarded Roe v. Wade as settled law. (The sixth never acknowledged this.)

The Dobbs decision directly impacts the right of any U.S.-resident person who can become pregnant to make decisions about their own body. It claims unjust authority over that body's movement through our tired, contracting, beauty-veined world. And it compromises an individual's ability to locate their own flourishing and happiness, which may stand single, among family, friends and partners, or eventually include the chosen addition of a child or children.

If you're reading *Our Beautiful Reward*, you probably already agree with all of the above. You may also agree that the struggle for reproductive rights is linked to other contemporary struggles for bodily autonomy, including trans rights; disability rights; the right to be free of violence both institutional and private; the right to not have the environment damaged so deeply that you, an embodied person, can no longer take care of yourself and others within it. Many affiliated efforts in the direction of justice follow from these beliefs.

In some of the writing that follows you will find powerful evidence of shock, anger and grief at acts of reckless authoritarian intrusion including, but not limited to, the overturn of Roe v. Wade. Not every piece in this collection aims to be 'constructive.' We have held room for fury and disorientation. In other works, you will find speculative approaches to living fully, defiantly, within threatened contexts. A good number of these poems and stories acknowledge that *for now*, freedom—that difficult-to-quantify, wrestled-over term—is felt and found from moment to moment, day to day, rather than existing as a great and secure continuity of unquestioned fact.

What we hope we have done in bringing these authors and works together in this special issue of *Reckoning* is to confirm that many of us, across the world, are working wherever possible to extend those moments, those days. Join us. Read on.

Catherine Rockwood (she/they) lives in Massachusetts with her family. Their poetry appears in or is forthcoming from *Moist Poetry Journal*, *Strange Horizons*, *Scoundrel Time*, *Contrary Magazine*, *Rogue Agent Journal*, *Lady Churchill's Rosebud Wristlet*, and elsewhere. Her chapbook, *Endeavors To Obtain Perpetual Motion*, is available from The Ethel Zine press. Another mini-chapbook, *And We Are Far From Shore*, is forthcoming from Ethel in 2023.

After the Ban

Linda Cooper

left eye the moon/chewed and spit across the sky

right eye a slender girl/leaning on a lamppost/her body newly claimed

neck hands/uninvited/ !

nose seven starlings wheel across the sky/bear her weight

hair wild horses/meandering attention/the half-life of respect

lips curl of waves/a flag/or a siren

ears silence packs its bags and disappears/the time to listen

chin she is becoming a hawk/comet/wall of fire

Linda Cooper lives in Ronald, Washington and teaches creative writing at Washington Outdoor School. She completed her MFA at Eastern Washington University and her poems have been published in *Verse Daily*, *Hayden's Ferry Review*, *West Branch*, *Many Mountains Moving*, *Willow Springs*, *Third Coast*, *Tupelo Quarterly*, *Los Angeles Review*, *Permafrost*, *Hubbub*, *Elixir*, *Diner*, *Pontoon*, and many more. She also won the 2015 Orlando Prize for Poetry and the 2022 Allied Arts Foundation Prize.

On This Day, and All Days, I Think About What I Have Lost

Dana Vickerson

On the day my son is born, a summer thunderstorm stomps and slashes through San Diego. Pellets of hail hit the window four floors up as I lie in my hospital bed and hold my squirming pink infant.

My husband checks the radar on his phone, making little comments to himself about unprecedented weather patterns and hook formations. Our son's face is a red, squishy orb, but as I gaze at him I can see my husband's cheeks, his eyebrows.

I fall asleep with my son at my breast, and when I wake my husband is holding him near the window. Night has fallen.

"The storm put out the fires," he says, his voice full of awe. "We're looking for the stars."

I join them at the window and the three of us look out at the June sky, wondering if the smoke will finally clear. The city's glittering lights dull the expanse of stars above us, but I know they're there all the same.

On the day my son turns two, we host a birthday party in our scraggly back yard. The kids from his preschool class run through our too-tall grass and climb on our splinter-riddled treehouse. The other parents sip light beers and eye us with curiosity and pity. They drove here in pickup trucks, SUVs and luxury cars. We share a beat up Forester that is older than our marriage. They ask what brought us to Dallas, and like most transplants, we say work. They regale us with Texas pride, and we smile and wonder if like their children and their cars, everything really is bigger here.

Planes pass overhead every few minutes, making their way to and from Love Field and DFW Airport. They seem to be increasing in frequency, and I wish we'd looked at flight paths before buying our house.

The father of the ginger-haired boy digging holes in my vegetable garden pulls me aside to ask for directions to the restroom. I send him into the house and notice he's openly carrying a pistol.

I catch him when he returns and ask him why he thinks it's appropriate to bring a gun to a toddler's birthday party. He looks at me with a hardened face.

"To protect my family, of course. Can't be too careful." He pauses, and I know he's trying to gauge if I'm like him or feel threatened by him. I ask him to leave.

I kick at a pebble in a muddy patch of the lawn as the man collects wife and son and goes without incident. Sweat slides down the back of my legs into my sandals.

The summers feel hotter here than anywhere I've lived, so I'm thankful the fat, gray clouds have blocked most of the sun. The children look pink all the same, and I think I should have bought juice boxes, even if the plastic cartons feel wasteful.

When our son is in bed, my husband finds me in the backyard braiding dandelions and looking up at the wide night sky. The clouds have parted. I spy early June constellations, though their brightness is faint even in the suburbs. He wraps his arms around me and kisses my neck.

"Will we be ok," I whisper to him, and I feel his body tighten around me.

"Us?" he says. "Always."

"No," I say. "The world."

On the day my son turns five, we're in the Forester driving north to Colorado with a trunk full of camping supplies. We plan to find a spot of Earth to claim for the next week, where we can see the stars unadulterated by the glow of civilization.

My womb is still bleeding from the final miscarriage that sealed our fate as a family of three, but I will not be deterred. I want to dig my feet into cool dirt and get lost counting bright dots of light in the milky sky. I want to get away from the preschool moms who won't stop asking me who I'm voting for in November and the protests and demonstrations that roil the city.

My son pulls on bright pink headphones and turns on his Switch, and my husband tilts his head toward me, eyes on the road.

"The San Diego office has closed indefinitely, so I won't have to go out there when we get back."

"Really?" I say, relieved.

He nods, his gaze distant. The sun irradiates the blacktop and wavy heat pours off the surface of the road. I'm anxious to begin our climb into Colorado and feel the cool breeze that comes with higher elevation, but part of me is afraid the heat will follow us. The vegetation along the road is parched and brittle. It looks ready to ignite.

"Yeah," he continues. "They don't want people leaving their homes. I guess the air quality is that bad."

I nod my head and think about the YouTube video I watched two days ago, long-burning fires tumbling down the mountains like ravenous wolves, consuming everything indiscriminately. Post office, grocery store, football stadium. I feel thankful we left when we did, but I do not feel relieved.

On the day my son turns eight, I call home to tell him happy birthday and let my husband know I've arrived in DC safely.

He is quiet on the phone, struggling with his desire to have me there versus his unwavering support as I make a last ditch effort to claw back the rights that have been eroded.

I scream and chant all day, and when night falls over the Capitol I sip beers with three girlfriends from college who all left their families to come to the city and add their voices to those of the women who still want the right to choose, the right to protect their livelihood, the right to vote.

I try to find the Big Dipper as I lift the cold glass bottle to my parched lips, but the air is so clogged that even the brightest constellations have gone dark.

I think about my boy, who is sensitive and loving and so much like his father, and I wonder what they're doing. I think about calling home again, but I don't want to hear my son's disappointment when he tells me about his day. He would never say he wished I'd stayed, but I know he feels that way all the same.

The next day the National Guard sweeps into the city and shuts down all protests. Tens of thousands of people—the ones who are not arrested—flee home. I am not arrested, but I take a can of tear gas to the face and am forced to stay for two more days at a local hospital for surface burns.

As I try to dial home that night, a ravenous summer storm descends on the city and takes out all power and cell service.

On the day my son turns thirteen, my husband leaves and never comes back. We have been hiding out in a friend's basement for two months, hoping the militia will not come through and conscript my son and husband, but my husband can no longer cower. He has a plan.

Thirteen is the age of readiness, the camo-clad terrorists say. They will take my son and put a gun in his delicate hands, and I will never see him again. The thought crushes my soul into fine sand. We should have left before they closed Dallas down, but we were under a cloud of denial that things would never get this bad, that there were enough of us to vote and protest and change the tide.

If we'd gone back to California before the Pacific States closed their borders, we would have had droughts and fires and protests there just the same. By the time we knew we needed to go, it was too late.

Our friends have a home full of daughters, and that carries its own risk, yet they keep up appearances to keep us safe. Their home is goodly, Godly, and open to the cause. They do not tell the soldiers who come in to appraise the lovely girls who are not quite old enough to be married off to go to hell, because that would end in bloodshed. The father has multiple sclerosis, so the militia lets him stay and watch over his family for now. When night falls, the city goes dark. Power rationing has been in place for the past year, and when it's safe to sneak a peek through the windows we see a sky erupting in constellations. Every look feels like a risk and an act of defiance.

My husband puts on a frayed backpack and tucks a pamphlet into his pocket. He tells me that his contact can get us out. There is room for us on the dairy truck that will deliver supplies to outposts in the east. The northern resistance is watching the routes and knows of the plan. They will intercept the truck and liberate us, and we can start over again in Pennsylvania. It's all set up. He just needs to make this run, secure our spot with the last bit of money from our savings.

He kisses our son on the head and wishes him a happy birthday and tells us both he'll see us by daybreak.

A month passes before I pull myself together enough to make my own plan.

On the day my son turns fifteen, I ride in the back of a pickup truck on the same highway we drove to Colorado when my son was five. I am surrounded by other middle-aged women, and I am alone.

Fires blaze in the grasslands. I haven't seen a clear blue sky in months. Lazy June heat is a thing of the past, and now the planet burns with the intensity of an oven well before what used to be winter comes to an end. We're wrapped from head to toe in light, white clothing, because if the sun does make its way through the pollution, it will sear our skin to blisters within an hour.

The truck rattles, and the women hold onto one another, some crying, some drinking from dented tin canteens, some trying to sleep. We are being moved to a shelter across the border. We are the lucky ones. We have been saved.

Dallas burns behind us as we drive north, the fighting still audible in my ears and heart. I wonder if my son is alive or dead. I have not seen him in eighteen months, since he was pulled from our shelter and loaded onto an armored truck with a handful of other boys and my friends' three daughters.

The militia had little use for a woman my age, but two months later they took me all the same. They were not good men. When I was lucky, the soldiers pretended I wasn't even there. I felt like a ghost walking through a ravaged world, and I howled at night for everything I'd lost.

Some part of me wonders if I ever had anything in the first place. If I had ever been carefree, or if I had been doomed from the start. I cannot remember now. All my memories of my son and husband are tinged with the background noise of news reports on the radio, comment threads on Twitter, and increasingly violent weather.

I try to remember my son's seventh birthday, what he wore, where we were, what he got as a present, but all I can remember is that I wanted to make him a chocolate cake and couldn't. The cacao crop had collapsed that year, and even if I could have found chocolate, I wouldn't have been able to afford it.

I lay my head on a gray-haired woman from Austin who lost her wife and two sons. Unlike me, she knows her loved ones are gone from this world. I don't know if I should pity or envy her.

She is stoic and never cries when she tells me about the organic farm she ran for fifteen years before the soil turned acrid and her plants died. She and I talk wistfully of tomatoes as the truck lumbers on to our salvation.

On the day my son turns twenty-one, I take a mug of homemade wine out to the porch of my tiny cabin and look to the stars.

The sky is wide open, ringed on the edges by mountains that lurk silently in the distance. The stars are brilliant and provide an ambient glow that illuminates the swaying grasses that surround my little home.

My Australian shepherd is my sole companion, and he twitches in his sleep as he lies across my feet. I wonder what he dreams about.

My dreams are cruel. In them, the world goes on unbroken. I watch my son grow up, looking more and more like his father every day, dark brown hair with streaks of amber that catch the light as he learns to ride a bike, learns to build a computer, learns to fall in love.

In my dreams, I hold my husband's hand as our son walks across a graduation stage. The high school is used for learning, not stockpiling weapons and triaging wounds.

In my dreams, my son brings home a boy, shy like him, taller than him, who holds his hand and smiles at my son with love in his heart and dancing light in his eyes. We help them move into their first apartment, drive their belongings down the long stretch of nothing highway between Dallas and their new life. In the old Forester on the way home, I cry, and my husband tells me that everything will be fine as tears roll down his face into his graying beard. We both know that the pain we're feeling now is just the untethering of our family of three.

In my dreams, my husband and I come home to an empty house, and for a long time we're sad and unmoored and there is too much time and not enough teenage angst, music at all hours of the night, or laughter. There is too much food in the fridge without our son to eat it all up.

In my dreams, my husband and I slowly come back to one another, back to the life we had before our son came screaming into this world on a stormy June day. We build a fire pit in the backyard, and though the city has grown around us, night sky ordinances dim the surrounding glow and open celestial views above. We sit outside and smoke a joint and try to identify all the constellations. Planes still pass overhead, but we have grown used to them.

In my dreams, we drive west into the nothing, into the vast land between Dallas and New Mexico that still hasn't been built up, no matter how much the world continues to prosper. We park our car on the side of the road and spread a blanket in the dirt and make love under a huge milky sky, the stars dancing with us and around us. We get back in the car and keep driving.

In my dreams, we go back to California. The fires have stopped. The revolutionary legislation passed just in time pulled us back from the brink, and now the rains have come back and the storms have subsided and we start an organic farm and spend our days with our hands in the dirt until our aging backs scream for rest. We eat butternut squash soup and sip chilled sangria and take long walks through our orchards at night, the stars and lighting bugs as company.

In my dreams, my son and his husband fly out to spend time on the farm, and with them they bring a squalling, squishy-faced baby that has my husband's cheeks and eyebrows. I bounce my grandson on my knee while I watch the men in my life pull cucumbers and tomatoes for our dinner, and I think of how grateful I am to have clean air and clear skies and a life of unburdened possibilities.

Though I know the heartbreak that waits for me in my dreams, I fall asleep on the porch as my shaggy dog warms my feet. When I wake the next morning, I'm cold and stiff and go into the house to make a warm cup of mint tea.

Fat, fluffy clouds make their slow crawl across the open Colorado sky as I weed my garden. I plant crops to harvest in the fall, potatoes and squash that will keep me and the dog fed through the winter.

Not a single plane passes overhead, and I wonder if some day they'll figure out how to produce enough gasoline again for air travel. I hope not.

I stand up and stretch my back and notice two figures walking up the long path to my cabin. As they get closer, I see they're wearing US Army fatigues, and sunlight dances off the amber shades in the younger one's hair.

For a moment, I think it is my son and husband, but of course it's not. The soldiers bring me a crate of supplies, issued to all homesteaders once a month. They know me, and I know them, and I offer them mint tea before they head on to the next farm.

I sit in silence with them, relishing the company, then I work myself for the rest of the day and wait for sleep to take me home once more.

Dana Vickerson is an architect and writer living in Dallas, though she's most comfortable deep in the woods where she loves to sit and listen to the symphony of nature. When not crafting buildings or stories, Dana can be found analyzing horror movies with her husband or making elaborate paper dolls for her daughters. Her short fiction appears in *Zooscape*, Dark Matter Ink's *Human Monsters*, Apex Magazine's newsletter and many other places. You can find her on Twitter @dmvickerson.

fertile week

Leah Bobet

the peas are in the ground and maybe it'll work
this time. I kiss your shoulders and crack jokes,
one day on, one day off, just like our doctor said,
and when the clock reads 11:11
our fingers twine, and we hold on so tight.

downborder, they're stealing bodies: put her in the dirt
and chant the words, she'll do your furtive will. a million
Murder Legendre brides reduced to flickering black and white
haunted house inspections; a million colonial possessions.
downborder, they shackle women by the waist in case we miss the point.

it took us so long to be ready for this.
to feel it turn to bullets under my lips.
when i took your hand, my hand was mine.

it's been a greyling spring, all rain, no relief in sight:
one day on and one day off. this year I'll build a trellis
so the soft green leaves can climb, pea tendrils curious
as new fingers stretching wide. this year I build walls
that are secretly ladders, designed to overcome,
strategically constructed to let in the sun. to let you in,
chin high, arms wide, precaution circumspection set aside,

all of us waiting through the blood-daubed protest signs,
craning necks over knees to the flickering screens
waiting breath-held as the baton moves inside
to be cracked across the face with an open-handed joy.

Novelist, editor, and critic Leah Bobet's novels have won the Sunburst, Copper Cylinder, and Aurora Awards, been Ontario Library Association's Best Bets, and shortlisted for the Andre Norton Award. Her short fiction has appeared in multiple Year's Best anthologies and is taught in high school and university classrooms in Canada, Australia, and the US, and her poetry appears in both speculative and literary journals. She was a founding editor at *Abyss & Apex*, editor of *Ideomancer Speculative Fiction*, and guest poetry editor for *Reckoning: creative writing on environmental justice*'s 2021 issue. She lives in Toronto, where she makes jam, builds civic engagement spaces, and plants both tomatoes and trees. Visit her at www.leahbobet.com.

Ghazal for freshwater—wai

Laurel Nakanishi

Not so long ago, my baby floated in amniotic wai.
Oceans within oceans, and beneath them—wai.

Kunawai spring makes a way through concrete,
beneath streets, alongside apartments, burbling wai.

Double the word for water in Hawaiian and the sum
means: goods, value, worth, wealth, importance—*waiwai.*

At Red Hill, the US Navy stores 200 million gallons of fuel
above the aquifer. A war machine knows no sacred wai.

A gasoline smell in the water. Then illness—vomiting, aches,
burning skin, diarrhea—5,000 sick from petroleum-laced wai.

Perched over the same aquifer, I fill my baby's sippy cup
with questions, *Is this, too, poisoned wai?*

Divorce water from its wealth and the words are:
expendable, collateral, justifiable sacrifice of wai.

Are we doing any better with these wells and pipes?
Our endless appetite for lawns and showers. Municipal wai.

O, do not make me lie to my baby. Let what is good, be good—
this gift of water, this person you love most, wai.

Navy says operator error was the cause of a May fuel leak from the Red Hill Storage Facility[1]

Laurel Nakanishi

O'ahu in May
the island

Red

none of it
water

1. Hawai'i Public Radio, October 27, 2021

Laurel Nakanishi is a writer, educator, and author of the book of poetry, *Ashore*. She was born and raised in Kapālama on the island of Oʻahu, Hawaiʻi. She holds degrees from the University of Montana and Florida International University, and has been fortunate to receive fellowships from the Fulbright Foundation and Japan-US Friendship Commission. She teaches creative writing to young people in Hawaiʻi public schools. www.LaurelNakanishi.com

Law

Robert René Galván

> *And priests in black gowns were walking their rounds,*
> *And binding with briars my joys & desires.*
> —William Blake

At first, laid down on clay tablets
like the footprints of a slender bird,
then, progressed through dried skins and pulp,
burgeoning past parchment
to a flood of writs so numerous
as to be incomprehensible—
mulled by the nine
in their archaic robes,
        most prefer dead stone
        to a living vine.

Robert René Galván, born in San Antonio, resides in New York City where he works as a professional musician and poet. His collections of poems are *Meteors*, published by Lux Nova Press, *Undesirable: Race and Remembrance*, Somos en Escrito Foundation Press, *Standing Stones*, Finishing Line Press, and *The Shadow of Time*, Adelaide Books. His poetry has been featured in such publications as *The Acentos Review*, *Adelaide Literary Magazine*, *Azahares Literary Magazine*, *Gyroscope*, *Hawaii Review*, *Hispanic Culture Review*, *Latino Book Review*, *Newtown Review*, *Panoply*, *Prachya Review*, *Sequestrum*, *Shoreline of Infinity*, *Somos en Escrito*, *Stillwater Review*, *West Texas Literary Review*, and *UU World.* He is a Shortlist Winner Nominee in the 2018 Adelaide Literary Award for Best Poem. Recently, his poems are featured in *Puro ChicanX Writers of the 21st Century (2nd Edition)* and in *Yellow Medicine Review: A Journal of Indigenous Literature, Art and Thought.* His poems have been nominated for Best of the Web and the Pushcart Prize. His poem, *Awakening*, was featured in the author's voice on NPR as part of National Poetry Month in the Spring of 2021.

Wild Winter Rose

Anna Orridge

Ben and Theo found Eliška's name funny at first. "*Delicious Elisshhhhhka*" Ben sang, with a pop diva-style vibrato, using a lightbulb as a microphone. His brother laughed. Eliška did too.

For a while after that, the boys called her Deli. But their mother, Mrs Trevalyn, told them not to. She said the name was undignified. "Our maid is not to be treated as a pet."

Eliška was certainly not treated as a pet. Nobody stared slantwise at a pet, the way Mrs Trevalyn did at her, with a sort of guilty disdain. She told the boys to call her Eli, which Eliška hated.

One morning, Mr Trevalyn looked at Eliška, arms crossed, as she made coffee.

"My wife thinks you're looking peaky, Eli. Are you okay?"

Eliška did not know what 'peaky' meant. She'd learned some English at school, but not enough to follow fast conversations and certainly not enough to understand words and phrases that stood at a distance from their meanings.

"I do not feel too bad. It is hard for me to sleep, that's all."

But she had caught a few glimpses of herself in the huge windows she spent so much of her time polishing. And what Mr Trevalyn said was true. There were smudges beneath her eyes, like the dark underwings of a moth. And she often felt nauseous.

Her life, however, was not without pleasures. Theo, the quieter and younger of the two boys, had decided to appoint himself her English teacher. He had even created a special classroom corner in his bedroom, with a blackboard and chalk. Eliška sat alongside his cuddly toys, cross-legged.

He read her stories, and got her to write up little rhymes on the blackboard. *Fee-fi-fo-fum I smell the blood of an Englishman.* He giggled as she got off the floor and chased him round the landing, stomping like a giant.

Theo found a picture of a skeleton in a magazine and they took it out and labelled every part. Eliška particularly liked the names of the bones in the foot: *tarsals, metatarsals, phalanges*.

Mr Trevalyn discovered them doing this and smiled. "Eli isn't going to need to talk about foot bones, Theo. She'd be better off learning about things in the supermarket."

Theo shrugged. "I don't talk about Egyptians or bar graphs much, but I'm still learning about them at school."

Mr Trevalyn laughed and ruffled his hair. "Very true, little man. You're an old soul."

Eliška took Ben and Theo to school each day, jogging along behind them as they zig-zagged on their scooters.

At the school gate one day, she overheard two of the mothers, who were from Czechia, talking about her. The way they talked was different from hers, but she could make out what they were saying.

"Is Eli okay, do you think? She hardly talks. I suppose it's just lack of English."

"She's got a learning disability. Selective mutism, I think they call it. Christ, wish my kids had a bit of that...."

They both laughed. But then one shook her head. "I'm bad. Shouldn't be talking like that. I don't like the way she's treated, to be honest. Exploitative."

The other shrugged. "She's treated no worse than any other au pair, I reckon. We see her twice a day, every day, with those two boys. If she's really unhappy, she could run off any time she likes."

Alone in her room later, Eliška pondered this. What the woman had said was true, of course. She could run away. But where would she go?

One morning, she caught Mr Trevalyn looking hard at her again when she was at the breakfast table, pouring orange juice into the glasses. Eliška did not normally mind a steady gaze, but there was something about Mr Trevalyn's watery blue eyes that unsettled her.

"I meant what I said about looking unwell, Eli. You need fresh air," he said eventually. "We'll have you out in the garden for a change. The beds need trimming and prepping for Spring, anyway."

Mr Trevalyn was proud of the family garden. It had a swimming pool in the shape of a cartoon speech bubble. Beyond that, a lawn stretched out, dotted with islands of flowerbeds. Some of them were tilted on slopes, in a way she'd only seen in parks before or at funereal floral displays.

The lawn was nearly as large as the park her dad had been responsible for as a warden back home in Slovakia.

Just like her father, Mr Trevalyn mowed the lawn. Dad hated mowing, though. He used to make fun of her aunt Monika's manicured lawn.

"If there is a God, Eliška, I can tell you now that this unfathomably complex being does not love tidy gardens. They will smite the shit out of any astroturf. Trimming borders of various kinds will not constrain those demons of your mind, or the silken voices whispering to you that there is more to life than spraying things and cutting in straight lines."

Mr Trevalyn loved his lawnmower. It was one of those you rode rather than pushed. He looked as if he was tempted to giddy it up like a horse with a knock of his heels.

He gave Eliška a swift tour of the garden and of the beds he expected weeded.

Mr Trevalyn put his hands in his pockets. "I'll show you the wildflower bed. It's rather tucked away and a bit unsightly. But it's important to let nature have free rein somewhere."

Free rain? Surely the rain was always free, pondered Eliška. Back in Slovakia, she could never resist the urge to go out when it rained, stretch her arms out and let the drops spank her tongue.

People were longing for rain in London. It had been months since it fell. Although the lawn in this garden was green, constantly watered by sprinklers, most were parched and yellow.

Mr Trevalyn took her right to the back of the garden, behind the topiary.

This bed was quite unlike the others. It had lots of dead stems and dried thistle heads.

She gasped and pointed. "Look. Beautiful."

Amid the dead stems was a rose: deep scarlet, petals still fresh. Eliška lifted it to her face. The cool petals brushed her skin. The scent wasn't full and blowsy. It reminded her of the fragrance of bluebells—so fragile, you just caught a hint of it, but it seemed to elude your senses if you tried to breathe it in deep.

Mr Trevalyn grasped Eliška's upper arm, below her t-shirt sleeve. "Off your knees. You should have some gardening gloves on—you can get nasty things from soil. You'll end up dragging half the garden into the house."

Eliška quickly scrambled to her feet, but Mr Trevalyn did not remove his hand. He pulled her backwards. He was gentle enough, but she did not like the heat of his palm on her skin.

Finally, his eyes dropped from her to the rose. He shook his head. "Ridiculous, flowering at this time of year. Global warming, of course. You'd have to be stupid not to believe in it." He made a clucking noise with his tongue against the back of his teeth. "It's over-population. People having too many babies."

Eliška looked down at the grass beneath her feet. "You have had two babies."

Mr Trevalyn raised an eyebrow. "I don't mean in countries like ours. Anyway, no need to do any weeding here. The weeds are kind of the point. Just trim round the bed. Get rid of that rose, would you? Clearly seeded from another bed. It's not wild."

But Mr Trevalyn was wrong about the rose. It had broken through frosty soil and had a headstrong wildness in it that Eliška recognised and revered.

Eliška's dad used to tend the rosebeds at his park. When the blooms were about to wither, he would cut a few and take them back home to put in a vase. He always put them next to the same photo of him and Eliška's mother, from when they were on honeymoon in Venice all those years ago.

Eliška's boyfriend Ladislav would sometimes lean over to look at that picture.

"She was so much like you."

Eliška shrugged. She knew she should feel some kind of connection to that stranger in the photograph, smiling and leaning on a column, the hollows under her cheekbones deep as the fluted stone.

Eliška took Ladislav's face in both her hands, rubbed her thumbs against his skin as if it was fabric she was testing for quality in a shop. He flinched a bit and laughed. Taking her hands, he led her to the sofa.

The carriage clock in the glass cabinet above them ticked with its irritated urgency. But Dad was out at the park, and he would not be back home for hours.

After she'd dropped Ben and Theo off the following day, Eliška went out and weeded the two patches nearest the house first. Soon, the borders were neat little brown cliffs against the clipped green. Then she went to the wildflower bed.

The rose was now fully open.

Eliška would not tear it out of the ground. Nor would she take it to one of the regimented rose beds for re-planting.

She carefully dug it up, nestling its roots in the centre of her palm, and took it to a sunny patch of ground near the fence.

When she came back, she found herself focusing on an odd mound, about 3 feet tall, just next to the wildflower bed. Idly, she pulled away the weeds and scrubbed at the moss until she discovered what looked like the top of a column, with three slits still wedged full of soil. After five minutes more of scrubbing, it became clear it was, in fact, a birdbath. The bath was held up by a cherub, moss filling the dimples of its elbows and the belly button of its round stomach.

Later in the afternoon, Mr Trevalyn came out to find her. He laughed when he saw the bird bath.

"Oh, crikey. You didn't need to clean that up, Eli. I meant to throw it in the skip. It's a bit of a Gothic nightmare."

"Please don't take it away."

The words spilled out before Eliška could stop them. Her lips went dry. "It—it makes me think of the statues in the park where my father worked. There was one exactly like this."

Mr Trevalyn's face softened. "You can keep it there, if you really want."

Numb with relief, Eliška nodded.

Mr Trevalyn wiped his hands down on his jeans. "I hope you feel content, Eli. It's terrible the way some people treat their domestic help. We feed you well, don't we? You don't go without."

Eliška knew what was expected of her—nodding enthusiasm. She managed a wan smile.

Once she had finished her gardening for the day, she went indoors to the downstairs toilet. She pulled down her gardening trousers, breathed out hard. Still no blood. She was at least three weeks late now.

She'd always been irregular, but there was a tiny thorn in the back of her mind, and it would not stop needling her.

The week after Ladislav visited her, the Danube had burst its banks. It wasn't the first time it had happened, but it was certainly the worst flooding Eliška had ever seen.

For a while, cars kept driving on the road, ploughing through the water that sprayed out around them like white angel wings. But then the cars started to float. The water was murky grey and moving terrifyingly fast.

Mrs Hudec in the block opposite theirs started waving some clothes out of her window, trying to attract attention. When she caught sight of Eliška and her father, she beckoned for them to open their own window. They could only just hear her shout over the sound of the rushing water.

"Jan, my little boy, he's running a fever. His skin is clammy and he's going floppy. I need to get him to hospital. I've been on the phone now for half an hour, but I can't get through to the operator. Please."

Eliška knew, immediately, that her father would help this family. There was no point trying to stop him. The odd thing was he was not what you'd call a tender-hearted man. His gruffness did not have a soft centre. But he always had to help in an emergency. It was part of his nature.

He had a two-seater kayak, which they took out to the countryside when they went camping. Mrs Hudec was in a ground floor flat. If Dad could find a way to tie up the kayak, they would lower the child out from the window into the seat. The hospital was not far away.

Dad pulled on his boots and waterproof clothing.

"Never go into flood water unprotected, Eliška. You don't know what's in there."

Eliška could make a pretty good guess from the smell. Still, none of this worried her too much. Dad had always been good in water. Whenever they visited a lake, he always swam right to the centre, his strokes long and assured.

Still, she did not want to watch. She stayed in the kitchen as he made his way downstairs.

Just as she was about to turn on the kettle, she heard screaming outside—lots of people all at the same time.

By the time she got to the window, all she could see was her dad's blue kayak upturned on the grey water, spinning down what had once been their street.

Garden. *Zahrada* in Slovak—a word she had always loved. Its long exhalation made her think of a foamless wave breaking upon rocks.

Ben and Theo were out in the garden. It was March, but the thrumming heat made it feel like summer.

The boys splashed in the pool, diving off inflatables that now permanently bobbed amidst its turquoise ripples.

That was when Eliška could retreat to the wildflower bed by herself.

The birdbath, which she regularly topped up with water, had been a success. She sometimes left little balls of fat on the edge of the bowl. She knew not to leave nuts—Dad had told her that was dangerous and could make the baby birds choke.

Babies.

She thought about writing a letter to Ladislav.

He'd come to visit her a few days before Dad's funeral. He'd held her hands between his, massaged the thumb, and told her he was so sorry. But he could not look her in the eyes. And when she brought his hand to her breast, he flinched and got up from the sofa.

He had told her that she could call or write any time she wanted.

The wild winter rose had long since withered. But Eliška was glad it had had time to unfurl and feel the light on its petals. She had carefully picked it, taken it upstairs to her room and pressed its dried petals into her scrapbook, arranging them in in an arc, bloody footprints on the clear white paper.

If she'd had his address, she would have sent it to Ladislav.

After her father's funeral, Uncle Jan took her back to the big house he and Aunt Monika owned, up on the hill near the old TV tower.

Jan told her to wait outside for a moment, because he needed to make a call.

Eliška leaned against one of the columns, as her uncle's voice drifted out from the hallway.

"No, there's no possibility of her taking the flat over. Study's out of the question. Look, I know it might sound callous, but we don't want to be saddled with her. I know she's a sweetheart in her own way, but there's a danger she may never become independent because of her slowness. It's best for her to strike out on her own."

Eliška quickly pushed herself away from the column.

She had often been called 'slow', especially at school. Her reading books were never the same grade as everyone else's. She was not allowed to take exams before graduation like the other students. But in all honesty, she was glad of the exemption. There was no way she would have been able to sit at a desk with a pen twitching in her hand as she filled out line after line of writing and the clock ticked away inexorably.

Her uncle emerged from his study. He grasped her hands.

"Eliška, I am sorry. I know you must think Monika and I are very fortunate, but things are not great for us either. The floods have meant that two sites we were working on are now basically uninsurable."

She did not resist, but her hands lay limp in his, and she stared at him. He told her that London was still a brilliant place for a young person looking to strike out on their own. He had friends there—good people. A family. The husband was a councillor and businessman, his wife a conservator. They had two charming little boys and needed an au pair. It would be perfect for Eliška.

Eliška simply stared out at the great stretch of mown lawn.

Jan sighed. "What are we going to do, hmm?" he asked.

Eliška still said nothing, but she knew 'we' was not the correct word, not the correct word at all.

Mr Trevalyn asked her to dig a new bed next to the fence, because he wanted to put up some trellises and plant vines. It was a very dry patch of soil, so Eliška struggled to get the shovel down deep enough.

Mr Trevalyn watched her with that strange, unblinking attention she found so uncomfortable. "You've got the movement wrong—you need to get it in at a different angle...."

Without warning, he came up from behind and put his arms round her to grasp the shovel. He smelled of mint and just a hint of old sweat under a heady layer of deodorant. His hands shelled over hers, but Eliška let go of the shovel and wriggled free of him.

For a moment, they stared at one another. She ensured her gaze did not slip, as she stroked her knuckles.

"I'm sorry, Eli, did I press down too hard?"

"You can do this bed yourself," she said simply.

"I was only trying to...."

"Carry on trying without me."

She turned and walked away, straight into the kitchen where Mrs Trevalyn was putting icing on a birthday cake. It was for Ben for next week.

"Eli, could you switch the oven on for me, please?" she asked.

"Not Eli. My name is Eliška."

Mrs Trevalyn looked up quite sharply.

"I don't know why you're taking that tone with me."

"I don't know why you're not paying me."

Mrs Trevalyn crossed her arms, breathed out in a whistle through closed lips.

"Eliška, that's really not fair. We are keeping the money to one side for you in an account. People like you are easily exploited. Your uncle was very keen to impress that on me. It would probably be best to send your wages on to him."

"Why would you do that? The money is mine." Eliška was shocked by the speed and force of her own words. "I think I am pregnant. I need the money to stop it."

Mrs Trevalyn opened her eyes wide. "Pregnant?" She sat down next to Eliška, actually took her hand in hers. "Your uncle did not tell us."

She shrugged. "He did not know. Neither did I. But I need to deal with it, now."

Mrs Trevalyn's lips tightened. "It?"

"Yes."

"Eliška, abortion is no longer possible in this country."

"Then I must go somewhere it is possible."

Mrs Trevalyn shook her head. She put her hands on top of Eliška's. "You are so good with Ben and Theo. You would make a wonderful mother, you know. I mean, I'm sorry that a man has taken advantage of you...."

Eliška removed her hand from under Mrs Trevalyn's. "He did not take advantage of me. Not the way your husband is trying to."

Mrs Trevalyn smacked a glass bowl down hard on the table, so much so that it spun, making a terrible racket.

"This is not fair, Eliška. I know you must be in distress, but this is inexcusable, lying like that. Do you not understand the weight of false accusations, where they could lead? My husband is standing for political office. I'd have thought you would at least think of Ben and Theo."

Eliška had heard enough. She stood up, letting the chair scrape on the floor behind her.

"Believe what you want of him."

Mrs Trevalyn did not say anything more about her pregnancy, but Eliška found vitamin pills on her dresser—folic acid. She immediately flushed them down the toilet.

"We are going on holiday soon, Eli," Mr Trevalyn said, over the dinner table.

"Eli's coming with us?" Ben bounced up and down on his seat in excitement, but slowed down when the three adults at the table looked down.

Mrs Trevalyn coughed. "It would be a bit too expensive for Eli to come with us, Ben."

Theo slammed his fork down hard on his plate. Enough to make them all jump. "That's not fair."

"She *will* have a holiday of sorts—Eli, we would like you to take a break. No need to do any cleaning while we're away. There will be a labourer coming in, to do a mosaic at the bottom of the swimming pool. We only ask you let him in at 8am and let him out again at 11am. We won't expect him to work through the midday sun, because that's inhuman in these conditions. After he's gone, you're very welcome to go and take a few trips out in London. You should get to see more of this city."

"I do not want to see more of this city," Eliška said.

Mrs Trevalyn swallowed. "Well, you are welcome to stay in the garden and relax, in that case. As it happens, Jeremy is going to have a party when he comes back, to launch his candidacy for the election. You see all those potted roses we've bought?"

"Yes."

"Well, if you're feeling well enough, it would be good if you could plant them on the sloping bed nearest the pool, in this design…."

She showed Eliška a leaflet, which she knew was one from Mr

Trevalyn's campaign. In the corner was a small, open red rose.

"Roses in the form of a rose," Mrs Trevalyn said softly. "Quite eye-catching, I think. And we know you have such green fingers."

A fortnight later, just a few hours after the Trevalyns had left for the airport, Eliška was about to go out into the garden early to fill up the birdbath when the doorbell rang.

She answered to find a young man outside, who introduced himself as Haroon. He had large, gentle dark eyes and a nervous shuffle of the feet. He pointed at a van parked behind him, the trunk open.

"I'll need to carry few things to the back," he told her.

She opened the gate to the back garden and let him carry all the tiles though. Soon, he was on his knees, taking up the old tiles at the bottom of the pool, which had been drained.

Eliška made him some tea, then went off to do some weeding around the bird bath. As she was leaning over, she felt nausea lurch again in her stomach. She clung to the cherub's shoulder as she vomited, a hand on the stomach that was just starting to swell. Tears sprung to her eyes.

By the time she'd got back, Haroon had pulled up all the old tiles. They were in a pile at the poolside.

"You're a maid? An au pair?" he asked.

"I also clean, cook, do the gardening."

He whistled. "More like a housekeeper then. Hope they pay you well."

"I am not paid at all."

Haroon tilted his head backwards and blinked. "What do you mean? That would make you a slave."

The word 'slave' shocked Eliška like a slap.

Confused, she walked quickly to the bottom of the garden, to the wild flower bed.

"Eliška, I'm sorry. Please come back." Haroon sounded genuinely anguished, but she did not respond.

The next day, when she opened the door to him, Haroon immediately started to apologise. But she lifted her palms and shook her head.

"No. You were right. It's just that I was shocked. To hear myself described that way. But I should thank you. You told the truth."

His shoulders sank a little—perhaps in relief, but there was also pain. "In honesty, my situation is not much better."

"They are not paying you for this work?" Eliška was genuinely shocked.

"They pay, but nothing like what the work is worth."

"Then, why don't you leave?"

He sighed. "Come. I'll explain."

As she helped him carry a pile of tiles into the garden, Haroon told her that really, he was not meant to be here in England. If he was caught by the government, he would be sent back to his country.

"Don't you want to go back home?" she asked.

"Not as it is. There are people who would kill me."

"Because of your beliefs?"

"Because of who I am."

Eliška was not sure she understood this, but she nodded.

"It is strange," she said. "You are desperate to stay, and I to leave."

"To escape this family?"

"Because I have a problem which I cannot solve. Not here, in this country."

She brought a hand to her belly, and left it there, keeping her eyes on Haroon. His forehead creased, but then he nodded slowly.

"You need to get back to your parents."

She shook her head. "They are gone. My father, recently. My mother, when I was born. She died of a haemorrhage."

"That's dreadful. But it doesn't mean you will go the same way."

"Perhaps not. But I still do not want to be a mother."

Haroon nodded. "Then the Trevalyns should get that sorted for you."

"It's against the law here."

Haroon laughed at that—a short, bitter laugh. He brushed a hand against the tiles he was working on. "You honestly think that people who can afford *this*—this house, bright green grass year round, ceramic for the bottom of their swimming pool—cannot find a way? Do you think Mrs Trevalyn would carry a child she did not want?"

Eliska did not know what to say to that at all. She started to mark out the rose logo with tape on the sloping bed.

Once he had finished his tiling, Haroon came and watched her for a while.

"Why are you doing it in that pattern?"

She explained about the logo and the election.

Haroon smiled. "There are other patterns you could make. Come, let me show you."

Two weeks later, Eliška watched from the upper floor of the house as the Trevalyns' guests filtered through the back door into the garden. The Trevalyns had come in late last night from their holiday, and had not thought to check her handiwork. Hers and Haroon's, that is.

The guests, with their glasses of sparkling wine, were soon gathered round it.

Instead of the shape of a rose, the roses spelled out some words in a rainbow arc.

THE PERSON WHO MADE THIS IS NOT PAID

There was soon a steady hiss of muttering in the garden. Guests took out their phones and started taking photographs. Mr Trevalyn and a few very stressed caterers were soon ushering them back towards the back gate.

Eliška turned away from the window and waited.

It did not take long for her to hear Mrs Trevalyn's breathing behind her. It was, as she expected, rapid and angry. But there was no screaming, no throwing of possessions around.

"You will have what you want. There is a doctor I know, a good one. I have got you booked in and it will cost you all the wages we were saving up for you and more. And after that I want you gone. I don't want to hear from you again."

Eliška looked up at her for the first time. She was quite surprised to see the other woman's eyes were reddened.

"Tell me where to go and when."

Mrs Trevalyn pulled out a piece of paper. There was a time and date printed out, and an address.

Eliška knew she would go to Haroon's house first. He had left his address. And he said she could stay for a while, if she needed to. She'd probably need a few days after the procedure.

She had no idea what she would do after that. No point thinking about it now, she just had to pack.

She had, of course, already said goodbye to her beloved wildflower bed, even blowing a kiss to the bird bath cherub, which regarded her with its usual blank, mossy stare.

Just one last thing to do.

She took her scrapbook, with the pressed flowers, into Theo's room and laid it on his bed. She opened it on the page of the wild winter rose and wrote *To the best of teachers.*

She ran a finger over the dried rose one last time.

It too had been transported to a place it didn't want to be, but still flourished for a while.

Perhaps another rose would spring from the wildflower bed, its stubborn little cluster of truncated roots like a fist beneath the soil.

Anna Orridge was born in Birmingham and worked for 15 years as an EFL teacher in Spain, Bolivia and Slovakia. She now lives in Croydon with her family, and works for an educational charity, leading on sustainability.

Anna's work most often falls into the horror and clifi genres, and she had stories published in Retreat West's 'Nothing Is As It Was' anthology and Mslexia's 'Weather' issue. Her speculative fiction tends more to the dystopian end of the spectrum, and 'Backdrop', a nightmare vision of a deluged London escaping into nostalgic AR fantasy, was adapted as an audiodrama by Alternative Stories and Fake Realities. She has, however, also strayed into solarpunk, and 'A Reconciliation' was the winner of the Urban category of the Climaginaries short story contest. She won the #micropoem21 and 'Hot Poet' competitions.

Her essay for the Off Limits Press collection 'Divergent Terror: The Crossroads Of Queerness and Horror' is due to come out in 2023. Go to @orridge_anna on Twitter to discover more about her climate activism, writing and love of all things corvid.

Bosque Nuboso: Terra Firma

Taylor Jones

Terrestrial Bodies

Julian K. Jarboe

In the grove of trees there is total darkness, shrouded
by the curvature of the hills and concealed by the community
garden, the back of the baseball dugout, the stone wall
around the stone house. Why bother parking the car
when seclusion waits right there out in the open for us?
I teach you the practice before you learn the words.
I have dirt on my knees below the skin; I have a blanket of clover
pressed into the book of my hips, splayed with spine inverted.

In the hazel of morning, you are the only one allowed to touch my face
and I am the only one who can ask you to open your eyes. Adjust to the dark
and see where pale light remains in halo around the crown of the branches.
I'm surprised how softly you trill in your pleasure, breath harmonious
with the breeze, the insects, the distant world, the immanent earth.
You fell from the sky and now lie grounded in bliss and emptiness
and resilience. There could never be too much of you
or too long of a pause between questions.

Julian K. Jarboe is the author of the Lambda Award-winning collection *Everyone on the Moon Is Essential Personnel.*

Photo credit: Tony Tulathimutte

This is a romantic comedy

Dyani Sabin

On the phone, she didn't have to call it
danger. We all know how to flirt our way out
if you have to. Watch your drink, park under a light,
walk so you can see between the cars.

We held hands to leave, though they hooted
at us to kiss when they saw. But how else to
hide the shaking. Bruises on her ass, her
wrists, her thighs. She called them geography.

Bad joke. Lessons they don't teach in school, although
we all learned. We went to the movies. Watched a man
stalk his way past boundaries. A happy ending. Romantic
violins played. Violence behind sloppily applied foundation.

Driving home in the dark she told me something
I cannot tell you. Guess. But I made her pull off the
road. Fears like tears rolled down her cheeks.
There was never a way out, no map in the jockey box.

Just two trapped girls, seventeen at
midnight, stopped in the parking lot
of an autobody shop, jamming broken
hearts together, trying to be whole.

Dyani Sabin is an author of speculative fiction, poetry, and science journalism. Her work has been published in *Strange Horizons*, as well as *National Geographic*, *The Washington Post*, and *Popular Science*. You can find her haunting a cornfield, chasing ghosts on the endangered species list, or on Twitter @DyaniSabin.

Charcuterie

Annabelle Cormack

Square teeth gummed
with grey filament,
cuspid and bicuspid,
cleave open my clavicle &
peck out the heart like a wet pip
sizzling. A glut, a guttering, head
engorged and swelling like a tick. *Santé.*

It is our own fault, really.
Diligent hands decode our bodies
to a riddle of bone, leave us segmented
in painless pieces.

Can you stomach me
now? Stripped and stippled
with shotgun pellets, a redblack
razzle-dazzle. I once heard
the tale of a hunter crucified
on a roe stag's antlers and now
that stag watches from the wall,
its grinning vice of empty jaws
complicit as a mother.
Entrecôte, anyone?

I understand now, why the pigs
came to eat their endings
from the palms of your hands,
how you made us into something
red, something to be washed
down with sauvignon.
Auberge espagnole of a rib-eyed
daughter, take what you please, don't
be shy. The unplugged heart spits
& shivers, vomiting runnels
of white fat on the plancha.

They always ask for it *saignant*.

Annabelle Cormack is a poet, writer and Creative Writing graduate from Bath Spa University. Having grown up in the *Diagonal du Vide*, or the *Empty Diagonal*, France's very own "desert" characterised by run-down agricultural land and isolated ghost towns, Annabelle's poems focus on the beauty and brutality of nature and the way family dynamics can be impacted by the harshness of rural life. Annabelle is currently studying for her MA, juggling several chaotic jobs, and working on a YA novel about cheerfully amoral witches and unkillable kings.

A Question of Choice

Rimi B. Chatterjee

'What is the meaning of this?' Pradip Shankar yelled as five men with sticks burst into his OB/GYN consultation chamber. The receptionist screamed. She ran out the glass doors just seconds before a stick swung and shattered them to fragments. The two patients who were waiting to see him, Mrs Singh and Mrs Malkani, grabbed each other as glass shrapnel flew everywhere. One of the men turned to look at them and grinned. 'Leave now, *randis*,' he said. 'Or stay for the fun.' The two women took one look at his red grin and fled for their lives. Downstairs, Pradip heard the shrill screeching of his wife's pediatric patients. 'Spare them,' he muttered. 'They're innocent.'

'We know,' said the man. He raised his stick and smashed the monitor on the receptionist's desk with a quick, professional jab. The other men took care of the TV. Pradip stood there helplessly. 'Why?' he wailed. Then a huge figure barreled through the broken glass doors and kept going until Pradip was pinned up against a poster of a smiling mother and baby. 'Ramprolac is best for your growing boy!' the buxom mother seemed to be saying. Pradip stared up at his former friend and patient. 'Himmat Singh?'

Himmat Singh ripped Pradip's black-framed glasses off his nose and stomped them. 'I thought you were a good doctor,' he said. 'I thought you understood.'

'I do! I do!' Pradip whimpered as Himmat Singh squashed him into the mother's cardboard breasts. 'Tell me what it is that I should have understood!'

'*Guddu*,' Himmat Singh spat. 'You said never to call him *guddu*.'

'What?' Then a memory stirred. 'Yes, I did say that.' Pradip giggled nervously. 'It was just a joke. Your wife, Himmat bhai, your wife was apprehensive in the ultrasound room, it is her first time after all, so I tried to put her at ease. First babies tend to be small for their gestational aaaaaaaaah!' Pradip's head hit the wall as he tried to avoid the speculum in Himmat Singh's hand. It clacked like a raptor's beak under his nose.

'You told my wife he looked like a doll.' Himmat Singh shook him. 'My unborn son.' The speculum clattered on the tiles. 'She thought you were saying she was carrying a girl.'

'I never said that!' Tears squeezed out of Pradip's eyes. 'It was a joke! A joke!'

Himmat Singh snarled. 'I thought you were speaking in signs, to save your reputation, because the law punishes if you tell me what she bears. I thought you didn't want the taint, so I took her to another doctor for the work.'

A horrified realisation began to dawn on Pradip. 'Wait… you didn't… did you…? I hope you haven't done anything foolish, Himmat Singh.'

Himmat Singh roared. 'No redblooded man wants his first child to be a girl! So I took the stupid bitch to a hack, a sawbones, and said, "drop her belly". But guess what we found after the deed was done, eh, Mr I-Came-Top-of-My-Class-At Chandigarh-Medical-College?'

'You… aborted the fetus? No!'

Himmat Singh's eyes turned cold. 'You said you would look after my family. You said I would have children I could be proud of.' He straightened and dusted his hands. 'Now I want to make sure you never have the courage to hurt a father like me again. Daljeet! *Sajao isko.*'

Daljeet, a squat, ugly man in a misspelled Arsenal t-shirt, grinned. He came over and patted Pradip's sweaty cheek. 'Now we shall play football-football.' Two men shoved him into a chair. Daljeet stroked Pradip's left knee and drawled in the tones of a derpy commentator, 'Gooooaaaal!'

'Please, please, please….' Pradip gibbered as they took his left leg and stretched it over the fallen water cooler. Himmat Singh squatted a couple of times and massaged his stiff calves. Then he grabbed Pradip's jaw in his huge hand again. 'Listen carefully, you scum. If you ever practice medicine again, I will bury you and sell your lovely wife over the border.'

'Please, please, don't hurt me, I promise I'll make things right, just give me another ch….'

Himmat Singh grunted and raised his enormous sandal-clad foot. He stared into Pradip's terror-stricken eyes. 'Don't worry,' he said. 'I won't twist the bone. You'd make a pathetic cripple, anyway.'

Then the foot came down, and the lights went out.

'Ahhhh! Mummy!'

'Stay still, *ji*.'

Pradip struggled to open his eyes. In the chink of reality thus revealed, he saw his wife's hands wrapping a medical journal round his thigh and securing it with lengths of packing tape. 'That should stabilise the bone till we get him to the hospital.'

'Ambulance is here, madam.'

'Call the stretcher-bearers. He must be lifted carefully.'

'Priya! Help me....'

'It's all right, husband.' A hand grasped his. 'They've gone.'

'Priya!' He clutched her and pulled her to him. 'Simple fracture of the upper left femur,' he gasped. 'Blunt force trauma applied anterolaterally to the....' The lights dimmed and flickered.

'He's out. Lift him on three. One.... Two....'

He wanted to say he wasn't out, but the sudden pain made his teeth lock.

When he came round again, he was in a hospital bed. His left leg was in a sling. Priya was sitting by his bedside, reading a book titled *What Girls Need*. The window showed night sky above the Chandigarh skyline.

'Oh good, you've come round.' She looked up and smiled. 'We put a plate in your leg. Shivani wants to keep you for observation. You'll be discharged on Sunday if all's well. I've cancelled your appointments.'

'Priya,' he moaned. 'I am ruined.'

She wavered, then rallied and smiled again. 'It's a clean break, *ji*. It should heal without sequelae.'

'He said... he said he'd murder me if I ever practiced again.'

'Worry about that later.' She stroked his hand. 'For now you must rest.'

'Will you stay? Priya! Please... I need....'

She hesitated. 'I have my Study Club reading tonight.'

'But....' His other hand waved vaguely, trying to free itself from the coils of the drip tube.

'Shivani's on duty. She'll see you get the best care.'

'Is your club more important than your own husband?'

'All right, I'll text them.' She quickly typed a message on her phone, then she went back to holding his hand. A nurse came in, smiled at Priya, took Pradip's IV channel and pushed 2.5 mg midazolam into it, as Priya had requested. Priya waited for the drug to take effect, then got up quietly and left. She looked in at Orthopedics on her way out. 'Thank you, Shivani,' she said to her friend. 'Watch him till I get back.'

'Doctor Mrs Khair Bintam,' said Priya to the twenty or so young women sitting on rickety chairs in the little one-room shed. 'In her, we lost a champion. But we still have this.' She held up *What Girls Need*. 'Khair Bintam was a scholar of women's history at the Turkish University of the Humanities in Istanbul. Do you know where Istanbul is?' Some of the more eager girls nodded. 'She wrote this little book for her two daughters, Ayala and Lila. They were then teenagers, and they didn't understand why their mother was never home.'

The girls listened attentively. Most came from hard-scrabble backgrounds, and some were first-generation learners. Priya had begun this initiative after she'd met Rani, a sixteen-year-old domestic worker who had showed up at Priya's pediatric practice, twelve weeks pregnant and begging for an abortion. In vain Priya had protested that she was a 'child-doctor'; Rani had merely said, 'Yes, child-doctor, make this child go away. If you don't, it will finish me.' So Priya had had a word with Pradip, who had grumbled and objected and finally done a D&C. Then he had insisted that Rani get 'counselling' at the local *satsang*. Rani had shaken her head firmly. 'He forced me, that Bappa from the bus terminus,' she said. 'I was minding my own business. He did it. Give Bappa your counselling, not me.' Priya had wanted Rani to file a police complaint, but the girl had laughed bitterly. 'Me go to the police station? Hah! You want five cops to do what Bappa did to me?'

'I'll go with you.' But Rani hadn't answered, just taken the strip of antibiotics Priya had handed her and gone home without another word. Pradip had read Priya the riot act for getting involved, then washed his hands of the whole affair.

But Priya hadn't been able to forget Rani. She'd reached out to some of her wealthy friends from school and medical college, and they'd started the Study Club for Educational Uplift of Disadvantaged and Vulnerable Girls. Priya had then nagged Rani and a few other maids and nannies from her slum neighbourhood to attend. In spite of its grandiose name, it was little more than an after-hours training centre with a pair of donated computers and a couple of shelves of dogeared books. Here the kids learned to use spreadsheets, write emails and keep basic accounts. Priya had told them this was the way to a better life, and so far they hadn't disagreed.

Since it was run by Doctor Madam, the middle-class housewives who employed the girls gave them grudging permission to spend time there. Some of them complained that the Study Club made the girls 'uppity', but the wives and employers all agreed it was better than those church groups that were luring girls with promises of free food and education. On Friday nights some notable female leader in their circle would drop in to give a talk, usually a *yogin*, a doctor or a lawyer. This week it was Priya's turn.

'Khair Bintam had a husband and two daughters, just like many of you, but unlike you she was always campaigning and teaching and explaining, just as I am doing for you today. She wanted girls to learn and use their minds, to work and be productive. Her books inspired me to start this club.' She noticed with a twinge of disquiet that Sudha, one of the older girls, was grinning broadly, as if she knew something very amusing.

'But of all the Bintam books, I love this little one the most. It's written in the form of letters to her daughters, and each letter answers a question that one of them has asked. What does wealth mean for women? Is motherhood an instinct? Should I wear makeup? Whom should I marry? Can menstruation kill you? How do I know if I'm in love?' Priya smiled. 'All questions I wouldn't have dared to ask my own mother when I was growing up.'

'Me neither,' said Rani with feeling. 'Very quick way to get a thick ear.'

'Those girls are lucky to have had a mother like that,' said Rani's friend Radha. The others nodded solemnly. Sudha was grinning *and* fidgeting.

'Yes indeed,' said Priya. 'In the introduction, Dr Mrs Bintam says that the reason mothers get angry when questioned is because they've been taught that knowing too much is bad for girls. So, because they love their girls, they discourage them from learning how to ask questions. Even though they wish someone had answered their own questions when they were younger. They do this because they don't know any better.'

'But they always *say* they know better,' Rani snorted. 'All the time.'

'Actually, Dr Mrs Bintam says that the older women, the mothers and aunts, in a sense do know better, because when they were young, they were taken aside and taught a lesson. Then they were told, if you breathe a word of this, bad things will happen,' said Priya.

Rani's mouth hardened.

'So instead of answering questions, the mothers were taught

to keep secrets.' Priya tapped the book. 'It's all in here. But Dr Mrs Bintam decided she was tired of keeping secrets. She resolved to speak out.'

'And what happened to her?' asked Sudha. 'How did she die?'

Too late, Priya remembered that Sudha was a nanny, and that nannies watched television all the time, because they were stationed in front of it with their wards, feeding them, playing with them, bathing and dressing them. They didn't always watch the cartoon channels. Sometimes they got glimpses of the news. 'It was a very sad business,' she said. 'She… she was shot by unknown men. On the steps of her university, as she was going home.'

Sudha nodded sagely. Priya went on, unable to stop herself. 'They burned her body before the police could get there. On a pyre of her own books.' For days after seeing the news clip, she hadn't been able to sleep.

'No wonder.' Sudha pursed her lips. 'What a wicked mother to write such things! Strange men can read all about her daughters' monthlies? Haw.' The other girls giggled nervously. Priya cleared her throat.

Rani frowned and turned to Priya. 'I have a question,' she said. 'The family next door to ours has three girls and they're always crying and begging for food. They used to have five but the two eldest were sent away to some uncle in the country. No one's seen them for years.'

'So? Why do you care?' Sudha snapped.

'Let her ask her question,' said Priya, but Rani had jumped to her feet. 'I care! Someone has to! When our father left us—'

'Same old excuses! Trying to pretend!' Sudha also rose, fixing her with a stern glare. 'Everyone knows what you did, Rani.'

'I did nothing!'

'You care about those girls because you should have shared their fate! You're just like them! Piece of shit!'

Priya stepped forward. 'Both of you, sit down!'

Rani was flushed and close to tears. She thumped back down on her chair. Sudha twirled the end of her pigtail between her fingers, and took her time smoothing her dupatta as she sat. Priya said, 'Sudha, please do not disrupt the class. Don't you want to hear what is in this book?'

Sudha shrugged. 'My mother says, when I marry I have to pay for a hut and a scooter for the groom's family, otherwise I will get a man who beats me.' Sudha pointed at the book. 'Does it say where to find those things? I think not. And why is that?' She turned to the other girls and spread her hands. 'Is it because Doctor Madam's daughters never had to worry about getting husbands who beat them?'

Priya sighed and laid the book aside. 'Sudha, in my family, I have five elder sisters. My father could only marry off three of them before our dowries and wedding expenses bankrupted him. My fourth sister vowed never to marry. She nursed my parents through their last years. I always knew I had to study hard, get a job, find my own husband. And I was lucky. I met a man who told me, "You are a good doctor, you can make ten dowries if you want." He believes in me.' She smiled, filled with a sudden rush of tenderness for her stricken husband. 'There are such men, you know. They're rare, but they exist.'

'How did you get into medical college, *didi*?' asked Radha.

'I studied hard and scored well in the entrance test.'

'Huh,' muttered Sudha, and looked Rani up and down. '*You* can forget it, trashbag. The only entrance test you know is how to open your legs.'

'Sudha!'

She grinned and folded her arms. 'I will say no more.' They could all hear Rani grinding her teeth. Priya heaved a big sigh. 'All right then,' she said, acknowledging defeat. 'As Sudha is determined to be difficult today, we'll discuss the questions next time.'

'Why are you like this?' Radha hissed, but Sudha only laughed nastily.

Rani remained sitting as the others left. Sudha lingered in the doorway with her cronies. 'Now she's going to cry to Doctor Madam. Just see, buckets will come down.'

'Sudha, go,' said Priya sharply. 'Meeting is over.'

Rani got to her feet. 'I'm going too.'

'Stay, Rani. Don't lis—' Rani rushed away. Priya almost followed her, then remembered she had to get back to the hospital before Pradip woke up. She sighed, locked the doors and left.

Pradip Shankar brooded. His left leg, bound up in its brace, felt as though it no longer belonged to him. Like a failed and sullen traitor forced to go on living in the household of the betrayed master. He grimaced as his bare right foot brushed the rough surface of the bandage.

Himmat Singh was right. He was a failure. All through medical college, he had nurtured the dream of building India's future. Now even his own personal future was slipping through his fingers. He had joined medical school to get a career, but then something slightly shameful had happened to him: he had grown to love medicine for its own sake. He was supposed to be learning how to provide for his family and acquire status in society, not dream of utopian futures. But dream he did, all through his student years.

The world was in crisis, every news feed said so. Too many people were clogging up the works, from primary schools to metro stations. Mothers and their baby-hunger were a threat to world civilisation. He'd always known this, but until now, he'd never really had the leisure to examine the problem.

So what should be the solution? Himmat Singh had wanted a son: was that so wrong? Men want sons: they are our only chance at immortality, he thought, trying futilely to scratch his left knee. In the course of acquiring sons, fathers produce surplus children, failed attempts, so to speak. In other words, daughters. Daughters must be married: they can't be left lying around for random men to take advantage of and shame the family. Therefore, he thought, reaching for a notepad embossed with bouncing babies, the proposed solution must at one stroke decrease unwanted births and lessen the upward trend of world population in subsequent generations.

He wrote in a careful, rounded hand: 'Sons produce no babies. Therefore, in the long run, sons decrease world population.'

But how to achieve this outcome? He felt the edge of something slip past him, an idea so brilliant it took his breath away. Where were his old molecular genomics notes? He tried to rise and grimaced as his leg twinged.

'Priya? O Priya! Priya? Oho, have you gone deaf?'

Priya looked in at the doorway of his empty chamber. 'What is it, *ji*?'

'My old notes. Where are they?'

'What old notes?'

'From college! My special project!'

'I have no idea what you mean,' she said, 'but all your papers from before we were married are in the trunk in the back room. I'll tell Jasbir to bring it here for you. Why do you want those old things?'

'Because I am a man of science. No matter what Himmat Singh says, I am a man of knowledge and intellect. I topped my class; you were the second topper, Priya. How dare he forbid me—!' His voice had risen sharply. He began again. 'If I do not use my mind, I will die.

I will die, Priya!'

She came in and sat down beside him. 'No you won't. You need to rest and heal now. All this nonsense will blow over eventually. You know what this city is like. There will be new scandals, new feuds. One man's tragedy is a straw in the wind.'

'Priya, you do not understand. Himmat Singh is a fixer, a wielder of influence. His roots run deep into the sources of power. And I have hurt his most sensitive spot. He will not forget. As long as he lives, I am a dead man walking.' He grunted a bitter laugh. 'Or rather, a sitting duck. He has hung a padlock on my mind as surely as if he had slapped a court order on me.'

'Can you not explain to him?'

'I tried, that day when he trashed the place. He was too angry to listen then, and he will keep me away now.' He turned to her. 'Anyway, what can I say? I should have been wiser. It has only been a year since we set up our joint clinic, and now there is so much damage to pay for.'

'The insurance will cover it. And I still have my pediatric practice.'

'No! I refuse to live off my wife's earnings like a pimp. If I cannot practice medicine, I must find some other calling. That's why I want my notes.' He slammed a fist into the desk. 'No man of reason should have to suffer as I am suffering. I must fix it.'

'Don't be angry, *ji*. Have some compassion for the man also. He is angry because he is ignorant. If the common folk knew anything, they would be the doctors, not us.'

'Exactly! This country no longer respects learning. All it respects is wealth. And power. Hah! You remember I wanted to specialise in gene tech, but then I realised I would have to work in some government lab for a pittance. OB/GYN was my second choice, with much better prospects.' A manic gleam appeared in his eyes. 'Hmmm, maybe God is telling me something. Maybe I am meant for higher things.'

'That's nice, *ji*.' She patted his hand. 'I'll send the trunk up with your afternoon tea.'

'Hey Pradip!' Natwarlal Nehra roared. 'Look, boys, it's Pradip Shankar. Come here, you old sawbones. Bearer, bring another round. How's the leg?'

'Better,' said Pradip bravely, as he took a seat in the snug of the Punjab Achievers' Club and leaned his silver-headed cane, a gift from Priya, against the polished mahogany table. Shortly after setting up his clinic, he'd joined this club in the hope that it would bring him high-profile patients, and it had, but it has also brought him into Natwarlal's ambit, which was a mixed blessing. Natwarlal ran a vast commercial empire, although he affected a Gandhian humility in person, always scrupulously buying only the second most expensive whiskey on the menu.

There was a new face in the usual circle of Natwarlal's cronies, a fair and decidedly non-Indian face. Pradip tried not to stare. Natwarlal clapped him on the back. 'Meet Lesley Chen,' he boomed. 'We were just talking about you.'

'Namaste.' Pradip folded his hands and bowed.

'English, please. Lesley has only been here a few weeks. He's a big engineering man in Ramdhun Corporation of Singapore. He is invited to Vij Vaghela's pure veg parties and all. Very big man. Bearer! Whiskey, Pradip? Single malt of course.'

Pradip nodded. Lesley smiled. 'It's okay, Nattie. My introduction to Chandigarh was a big Punjabi wedding: my own, so I do know some of the words. Namaste!'

'You got married in Chandigarh?'

'Indeed he did!' Natwarlal roared. 'To Reshmi Arora, star of my favourite Punjabi soap!'

'Congratulations,' said Pradip sincerely. 'Reshmi is my wife's favourite actress also.' Lesley was blushing at all the attention.

Natwarlal barrelled on. 'I was recommending you to Lesley for consultation, Pradip, for when his lovely wife gets her good news, then I remembered your, ahem, problem.' He waggled an eyebrow at the cane. He leaned towards Pradip. 'No more trouble from that quarter, I hope?'

Pradip shook his head. 'He has not shown his face since.'

'And he won't. So long as you don't practice publicly. But in private… much can be done.'

'I've been thinking about that,' said Pradip. 'I have an idea. It is better than medical practice. It is really about what happens *before* my patients come to me.'

'Oho!' Natwarlal's eyes twinkled. 'You want to become a sex doctor?'

Pradip turned a furious red. 'No! I want to help men have sons.'

'Isn't that what you do already?' asked Lesley.

'No, I help women have babies. I do absolutely nothing for the fathers. That must change.'

Their drinks arrived. And then they had a very interesting conversation about Pradip's future plans. By the end of the evening, well lubricated with whiskey and veggie kebabs, Pradip was feeling more positive about his project than he had in weeks.

'My idea will work,' he muttered to himself as his car came round to take him home. 'I will show them all.'

'So what do you think?' asked Pradip Shankar.

Priya paged through the document, her gaze lingering first on this diagram, then on that. When she didn't respond, he asked with more acerbity, 'You do understand the science, yes?'

'Pradipji, you can't do this.'

'Why not? I said I would solve the problem of Himmat Singh. Is this not an elegant solution?'

'It's...unethical. You could be stripped of your licence.'

'*Uffoh*, don't worry about that. I have friends.'

'And... you can't call it a vaccine. Vaccines prevent diseases, and this... what does this prevent?'

'Poverty,' said Pradip Shankar. 'Overpopulation. Underdevelopment. Prostitution. Climate change. So many evils will be prevented by Humane Choice.'

'Climate change?'

'It is very simple, Priya. There are one billion people in India alone. If half of those people become mothers even once, that is an extra half-billion people in the next twenty years at least, overloading the planet beyond capacity. But,' and he raised a finger to forestall her objections, 'if the children of those mothers cannot have children themselves, the problem is stopped from growing. Ergo, those children must be males. We have to save the planet by having sons, not daughters. In one generation, we can reduce earth's population to manageable levels without any suffering or chaos. We need to have just enough daughters to keep the core population renewed.'

'The core population? But how will you—'

'*Uff*, Priya, you are so simple. The core of society is the families with the resources and the will to bring their daughters up correctly.' He fixed her with a stern glare. 'You of all people know how expensive it is to rear a daughter, not least because we must have security, surveillance and good staff to keep them safe. That burden will henceforth be only taken by choice.'

'Choice?'

'Fathers who want daughters can opt to delay the administering of Humane Choice until they have had them. They will be the lucky few in charge of creating the next, sustainable generation. Sub-par fathers need not burden themselves with girls at all. They can take Humane Choice straight away.'

'Sub-par?'

'If we restrict the production of surplus females, the ones we produce will be able to fulfil their sacred destiny as mothers without destroying the earth, and they will be treated as the precious resource they truly are. Thus our society can protect women, fathers will have the children they desire, and people will stop foolishly blaming mothers for giving birth to girls.'

'But what will—'

'This will eradicate the evils of dowry. More than seventy years of Independence and we have still not managed to do that. But now we will.'

'What about the mothers? Don't they get a say in this?'

'Of course they do. This is for their benefit. You know as well as I do that sex selection happens through the male contribution. Yet women are blamed for it, or they are forced to risk their health by bringing failed attempts to term. The government is at fault for this. By criminalising sex selection of fetuses before birth, they only spread fear. Himmat Singh thought I was talking in some secret code. Would this have happened in an enlightened country? Do you know that in US, they have parties when they find out the sex of the coming child? We are robbing our fathers of that privilege.'

'I know all this, *ji*. You don't have to convince me. But you cannot release a vaccine without undergoing clinical trials. There is a procedure.'

'Do not worry about all that. Natwarlal Nehra of NehraMed has agreed to arrange that part for me. They have hospitals and facilities all over the country. They will do the needful. But I have to make the requisite number of doses within the next six months and that's where I need your help. NehraMed Chandigarh has offered me a factory to make it. I need you to recruit the people, design the manufacturing process and keep the books. You are good at such tasks.'

She stared at the pages helplessly. 'You are going to use a carrier virus to deliver a payload to germline cells? What is this rAAVan? People will ask why you have maned it after the most notorious villain in Indian mythology!"

'It's the Recombinant Adeno-Associated Viral Analogue I am using,' he said a little sulkily. 'Never mind that part. This is a secret formula, protected by corporate law. The public will not see it.'

'Corporate... law?'

'Indeed, yes. Lesley explained how to do it. Ah, I forgot to tell you, I have made a new friend. See? I am expanding my circle, just like you asked.'

'Good, but—'

'His name is Lesley Chen. He is a Chinese engineer from Singapore, but he is here in Chandigarh building the new State Assembly Annexe for Ramdhun Habitat Projects. He is married to Reshmi Arora.'

'The TV star?'

'She is retired now. He wants a son. He helped me set up Humane Choice Private Limited. I will need your signature, you are also a partner. Lesley and Natwarji's legal team will bring the paperwork next month. You are agreeable, yes?'

'As you wish, but you really should have consulted me before you got into all of this. It looks....'

'Consulted you? Why?' Pradip's moustache bristled. 'I am the one Himmat Singh attacked. It is up to me to fix this. Lesley has been very helpful. I must take advantage of his contacts while he is here. Any day Ramdhun may order him back to Singapore. Reshmi wants to meet you. Also, I took the vaccine, so you may consider the human trials to have officially begun.'

'What!?'

Pradip looked slightly uncomfortable. 'They challenged me, Lesley and his friends, to show that my vaccine is harmless. So the last time I visited the Achievers Club, I took with me a dose from my first viable batch, and I injected myself with Humane Choice in front of them. To convince them.'

Priya stared at him. He made an irritable gesture. 'I would be a poor inventor if I did not believe in my own creations. In any case, Priya, we have vowed never to have children, so it does not affect us. My OB/GYN practice has been murdered in the cradle, but your child-doctoring is still alive. Unlike me, you are still a viable parent to your profession.'

'I would have... maybe... liked to have had a daughter, one

day,' Priya said in a small voice. 'But... I suppose we can still adopt....'

Pradip wasn't listening. 'Lesley wants a boy to share his triumphs and carry forward his legacy. He has been afraid to start because he can only afford one child, but I will persuade him. This will take the uncertainty out of parenthood for many, many men, all over the planet. They will not have to mortgage their present to pay for the future, they will have just the child they want, and they will not clutter up God's earth with extra women in the process.'

'What kind of world will it be if most of the children are boys?'

'It will be a highly productive, rational, go-getting and sane world, that I can tell you,' said Pradip firmly. 'Are you not tired of these teen pregnancies, trafficking, gag rapes and love *jihads*?'

'Do you mean "gang rape"?'

'Whatever. Too much drama. This vaccine is liquid engineering, Priya. All it does is tag X-bearing sperm and make them sluggish. They are somewhat like that anyway, because they are slightly heavier than Y-bearing sperm. My vaccine does not kill them: girls can still be born, just at a lower frequency.' He took her hand. 'Please be assured, Humane Choice does not break the law. Sex selection before birth may be illegal in India, but my vaccine is not to be given to pregnant women, or any women at all. There is no child who is being selected for or against. All I am doing is giving reproductive choice back to the fathers.'

'Are you certain this will be a good thing for the world?'

He patted her hand as it lay in his. 'I swear it.'

'Your husband is a murderer.'

Priya nearly dropped the book she was holding. 'Rani?'

'You heard me.' Rani came out of the shadows near the door. She picked up a duster and began helping Priya to dust and reshelve the library books in the Study Club's tiny book corner. 'Your precious Doctor Shankar is murdering our futures.'

'Do you mean Humane Choice? Oh Rani, it's not like that at all.'

'All the big men are getting it. No one says anything straight, but I hear them talking when I wipe their floors and wash their children's backsides. 'They say "Go to Dr Shankar, he will tell your husband to come for flu shot, then in three months you will get blessings." You think I don't understand it?'

'You have no proof.' Priya turned pale.

'Proof!' Rani sneered at her. 'Aren't you the woman who told us we should have dignity and pride in ourselves? Where is your pride?' She flicked the duster like a whip. 'You are helping him. It's your patients who are gossiping.'

Priya took a deep breath to object. But she couldn't let the words that crowded her mind come tumbling out of her mouth. Such disloyalty that would be. Finally she deflated. 'He's obsessed,' she said in despair. 'He asks me to point out the mothers who are sad because they had a girl. I tell them to bring their husbands, and he does the rest. But I think the husbands have figured it out. They have started coming to him directly. So don't worry, Rani, I am not helping any more.'

'Aren't you hiring people for the factory? And I hear you go there every day and sit in an office.' Rani wagged a finger at her. 'You're helping him, you liar.'

'He's my husband!' Priya wailed. 'He just does things, he never asks me.'

'And you go along with it? Where's your spine? Stop keeping his accounts and doing his dirty work.'

'He'll get someone else to do it.'

'Yes, someone he cannot trust. Someone who might steal all his money or sell his secrets.' Rani snatched the book out of Priya's hand and threw it across the room. 'You have to give us a chance, *didi*. You have to walk away.'

'How? He will never allow it.'

'Then help us. Radha and I and a few others have started our own group. *Kuri* Kommandos. We're going to fight him.' She puffed up her chest. 'We are Girl Kommandos and we will protest your Humane Choice until it is banned.'

Priya stared at Rani. Then she rose to her full height. 'Are you threatening my husband?'

'No, *didi*, I am asking you to help us. We have to shame him. Tell the world what he is doing. Show his evil. Only then will police do anything. And you.' She pointed an angry finger. 'If you do not help us, you are accessory!'

Too late, Priya remembered that Rani had a newfound taste for police procedurals, thanks to the watchlist of the latest family whose kids she was minding. 'You can't ask me to do this.'

'Huh. So you are fine with making and selling these death-doses?'

'That's not what this is. No one is dying. We are just… adjusting the future a little bit. Isn't this better than people abandoning their babies or feeding them milk laced with opium? And I'm not fine, if you must ask. I have doubts. I'd like to stop him, but he's shut me out. He only comes to me when he needs something. It's these new friends he has made, through Natwarlal Nehra.'

'Natwarlal Nehra! The King of Chandigarh?'

'Yes, him. My husband is a member of his club, and Natwarji has convinced Pradip that he must "think like a businessman" and acquire money and power. That way the Himmat Singhs of the world will not dare to touch him.'

'Your man is a coward. And if you help him, so are you.'

'Rani, please. Don't insult my husband to my face.'

'How can it be an insult if it's true? You live with him. If I can see it from where I'm standing, you can too.'

She sighed. 'So what do I do?'

'*Hai rabba!* Are you a child?' Rani clasped her hands. 'Stop thinking like a wife and think like a woman! What will the world be like if there are three Bappas to every Rani?'

'But he says the lower classes will have no more daughters. Only rich families will choose to have girls. There will be no Ranis at all, just Bappas.'

Rani's eyes flashed. 'Is that supposed to make me feel better? What am I supposed to do? Vanish? I have to live on this planet you are creating.'

'Oh, don't be dramatic. Surely having fewer girls will mean less trafficking and abuse? Your employers will have to pay you more, won't they? If there are fewer maids you will get more work.'

Rani stared at her, speechless. Priya shook her head. 'Look, Rani, I do know this isn't right, I just… I can't find a way out. I've tried so hard. Although… he did promise that I could retire from managing the company if Ramdhun Corporation buys it. Then we could go live in Singapore, and there would be no Himmat Singh to cause trouble. We could reopen our joint clinic. It would be just like old times.'

'Hmph.' Rani put her hands on her hips and glared at her former mentor. 'In that case, Doctor Mrs Shankar, my recommendation is that you pick up your worthless *tashrif* and get the hell out of my country.'

'Really, Rani? After all I've done for you?'

'You make me sick.'

'He is not returning my calls,' said Pradip Shankar, slurping his tea. 'That Vij Vaghela of Ramdhun. Lesley swears he gave the correct number of his personal line in Singapore. But he also told me the old man is doddering.'

'What shall we do, then?' Priya asked, laying a plate of steaming samosas in front of her husband. 'Is there any other way to reach him?'

'We could go there, I suppose.'

'Oh yes!' She brightened. 'Let's!'

'Hmph. It will cost a lot of money. And you will want to spend even more when we get there.' He cracked open a samosa and blew on his fingers. 'No, I have a better idea. I will ask Lesley for Mr Selvam Vaghela's contact number. I have a feeling that if the father is doddering, the son will be running things tactfully behind his back.'

'Selvam? What kind of a name is that?'

'His mother was a Tamilian. Foh!' Pradip scowled and licked his singed thumb. 'I ask you, are there no girls of good family in Gujarat?'

'Maybe they do things differently in foreign lands.' Priya went back into the kitchen to hoick more samosas out of the crackling oil.

'Well, they certainly have more sensible laws. None of this sex selection nonsense.' Pradip scooped the filling out of the samosa and left a messy pile of fried pastry crumbs on the side of his plate. '*Suno ji*, did I tell you I am writing a book?' he called to Priya in the kitchen. 'It will be titled *Future of the Child*, and in it I am going to explain all my ideas on how to save the planet and mankind.'

Priya reappeared, holding a spatula, worry creasing her brows. 'Is that wise? We don't want to draw attention to Humane Choice.'

'Attention?' His voice was incredulous. 'There are Humane Choice clinics in every major city in India. Five right here in Chandigarh. All built on a framework of trust and known only by word of mouth. My clients are the most loyal in the world. Now, I want to go global, and I will do it with or without the help of these Ramdhunites.' He waved her back into the kitchen. 'I was going to ask you to read it, but you are too busy keeping the accounts and running the factories. So Lesley is reading it now.'

Priya turned off the flame and brought the last of the samosas to the dining room. 'Is he still disappointed at the birth of his daughter?'

Pradip's brow creased. 'I explained to him, it is not a failure of the process. Some of us must take the hit and raise the next generation of mothers. And whatever he says, he can afford it. Ramdhun is promoting him to Head of Engineering.'

She nodded. 'Smiti is such a darling. I am glad Lesley has learned to love her.'

He shrugged. 'Very few of the senior execs at Ramdhun have children. Lesley is a traditional-minded man, which is why he and Reshmi get along so well. The others care only for career and parties.'

Pradip's phone rang. '*Jai Ramji ki*,' he said, clapping it to his ear with his left hand as he crumbled another samosa with his right. He listened and paled. 'Oh my god!' He listened some more. 'Just paint?' Someone spoke at length on the other end, Pradip nodded and hung up.

'What's happened?'

He looked at her sombrely. 'Some hooligans threw red paint on one of our downtown clinics. And they wrote "Murderer" on a patient's car: no one important, thank god. I am going down there now to make a police complaint.'

'No! Don't do that. It's nothing, and we don't want the police asking what we do in our clinics.'

'Why not? We are not breaking the law. Let them ask.' He got up to go wash his hand, then paused. 'Why are you always so scared, Priya?' he asked. 'You have so little faith in me?'

'I am beginning to suspect that what we do is wrong!' she burst out.

'Wrong!' He smiled at her indulgently. 'The planet is dying because of women's unstoppable urge to bear children. Alone of all scientists, I have stepped up to find a solution. I am a saviour, if I am anything.'

'Women don't have to bear children. I mean, I like them, I spend my days healing them. But I don't want to produce one of my own. I thought of adopting, but you hate the idea.'

'Adopting is just playing at dolls. You can't really care for a child unless he is your flesh and blood. I have seen this even with surrogate babies. The parents are never quite free of suspicion that the child is not theirs.' He patted her shoulder with his left hand. 'Anyway, that is not the point. Saving the planet is the point. It is cruel to expect women to forgo their essential biological function, ergo, we must have less women. Simple.' He headed to the washroom. 'I will take up this topic again at dinner.' She heard the sound of the water running as he washed up.

She poked the cooling samosas. She wanted her anger to

simmer down like hot oil taken off the fire, but it would not. When he reappeared, she said without turning, 'I know about the blog. "Priya Shankar Writes", it is called, but it is not written by me.'

'Oh that? Eh. I am just avoiding Himmat Singh. Surely you do not mind.'

She turned to face him. 'I forbid you to use my name to promote your ideas, Pradip.'

'You forbid me?' He laughed. 'But it is not your name, it is mine. If you insist, from now on I will sign my blog posts "P. Shankar". Is that good enough for you?'

Priya felt her right hand clench in an unforgivable gesture of rage and quickly hid it in her dupatta. 'Everything you do is based on the idea that women are—that I am—inferior to men. But you can't have it both ways. If I am nothing but a baby-making machine, how is it that I am running Humane Choice?'

Pradip burst out laughing. 'You! You just do the books and scold the staff. And answer the emails from clients. And make the schedules. I have the vision and the technology. I bring home the food, you cook it. You are labour, I am capital.' He flapped a hand. 'Put away these samosas, Priya. I have work to do.'

Rani turned into the narrow lane that led to her hut. It was nearly 2am and even the dogs were asleep. The one curled up just inside the mouth of the noisome alleyway pricked up her ears, saw who it was, huffed and went back to sleep. Rani hoicked up the two-kilo sack of potatoes that was slipping from under her elbow yet again and managed to get an arm round the bottom. Thus burdened, she shuffled along, occasionally scraping the rough brickwork and cursing. As she passed the only lightbulb in the winding alley, a shadow moved. Rani's breath hissed sharply through her teeth. 'Bappa? Get out of my way or I'll break your fucking nose.'

'It's me.' Priya raised the dupatta covering her face. 'I had to see you, Rani.'

'Doctor Madam!' Rani dropped the sack of potatoes and rushed to her. 'Is something wrong?'

'Yes. Everything.' Some of the potatoes had fallen out and were rolling towards the permanent streak of mud and filth in the middle of the alley. Priya quickly knelt and began gathering them up. Rani followed suit. When the sack was full again, Rani said, 'Let's get inside. It's dangerous for you to be here. If Sudha sees….'

'I was careful.'

Rani looked her up and down. 'Even with that faded salwar-kurta, no one would mistake you for a slumdweller. Come on.'

Inside the tiny hut, Rani lit a hurricane lamp and set it on a shelf. 'All right, tell me.'

'I've stopped helping him. Natwarlal has convinced him he needs professional managers, so he has let me go. I came to tell you.'

'You didn't have to. It has gone beyond what one person can or cannot do.'

'I know. I should have listened to you when you first told me. But… I was brought up to be obedient, to treat my husband as a god. Even though I knew before I married him that Pradip is no god.'

'Urgghhh! Finally!' Rani rolled her eyes.

Priya's eyes filled with tears. 'I loved my father. When my mother said he was an avatar of all that is good in the world, I believed her. I wanted a man like him to be my husband. For a while, I thought Pradip was that man. But now I think… now I think they are all flawed. Even Bapuji, who bankrupted himself for us.'

'God, you upper class women. All this education and you have less sense than silly little Radha. I want to bang all your heads together till your brains start working again. If they ever did.'

Priya smiled sadly. 'I deserve that. So I came to tell you, he is launching that vile book of his on Sunday afternoon at the Bollywood Book Nook on Harpreet Singh Avenue. Raya Advani, the movie star, will be releasing it, and all the famous people of Chandigarh will be there. I won't: I'll find some excuse. They will start at 5pm. There will be private security hired by Natwarlal Nehra, but they will be watching only for Himmat Singh's goons, not your girls. If you want to make the world pay attention, this is your chance, Rani.'

Pradip Shankar faced the glittering crowd that thronged the upmarket book cafe. This book launch was his big move to get Ramdhun Corporation to notice him, and he intended to make the most of it. Such a pity Priya had contracted a stomach bug.

Beside him on the dais, Raya Advani, Chandigarh socialite, rising actress and successor to Reshmi Arora, had just unwrapped a virgin copy of *Future of the Child*. The rows of social butterflies, suave intellectuals and well-heeled wellwishers drawn from his star-studded patient-base clapped enthusiastically. And now someone had asked him a question. The question didn't matter: he barely listened. He knew what he wanted to say.

'Viruses are not our enemies,' he said. 'Do you know that up to forty percent of the human genome is genetic material left by retroviruses? And that some of these retroviruses have donated viable and even necessary genes to us? Mammals arose because of a viral infection that caused the eggs of certain dinosaurs to stick to the womb lining and suck upon it like parasites. That should have been the end of those creatures, and I am sure many died, eaten by their own children. But there were some mothers so generous, so willing to give everything to their vampire offspring that they grew a protective layer over them and let the place of implantation swell and gorge with blood and food.'

The celebrities' eyes were glazing. This was usually the point where Priya would nudge him and murmur, 'No more, *ji*.' He ploughed on: Priya wasn't here to stop him.

'That was the rise of the placenta, and when the viral genome merged with the dinosaur genome and became an endovirus, it created a new kind of animal: *mammalia*, named for our ambrosiac innovation, the mammary gland, source of all beauty, sustenance and love.' He paused for a moment. Raya murmured, 'Shankarji, you are a true poet.'

He glowed. 'There is no human gene for creating this magical connection between mother and child. It is only this endovirus that makes happy families possible. We arose to conquer nature because of an ancient, indomitable infection. Viruses are not our enemies. They are our creators.'

They clapped a little uncertainly. Raya said, 'Shankarji, please tell us about your vision of the future.'

'Yes. As a rational species in the order *Mammalia*, we now have a duty to limit our numbers, since war and famine and disease no longer do so. That is the "Humane" part of Humane Choice. To do this, I have taken the help of a harmless virus that is naturally found in human semen. It is like a high tech postman, and it carries a message to the eager sperm: the Y chromosome wins the race!'

He chuckled, and the crowd chuckled with him. 'Not every time of course, because we must have some women. They make our lives so much brighter, and I might add, tastier. My wife, who is not here today, is a very good cook.'

'Wonderful,' gushed Raya. 'I love how you focus on the positives. The world needs hope more than ever these days.'

'Yes, my dear, there is hope. Friends, do not give your donations to the temples, go instead to the laboratories where the best minds of our nation are priests of the new—'

'Thief! Liar!' Girls climbed on chairs, wearing army fatigues with the words 'KURI KOMMANDOS' written in yellow paint on their backs. 'Murderer of our future! We know what you're doing!' Rani shouted. 'We demand to live! Let girls be born! We are not the killers of the planet. You are!'

'Guards!' Natwarlal's musclemen moved in to grab the protesters. But more girls were spilling in, raising posters over the heads of the stunned socialites. 'Down down Humane Choice! Down down Shankar!' In the street, glass shattered as girls jumped on parked cars and kicked the windows in. Two burly cooks in saris were beating a security guard with their posters till the flimsy wood shattered in their hands. Then they used their hands. 'Give us back our future!' Rani screamed. 'Give it now! Or we will take it!'

Rani picked up an encyclopedia and beat an industrialist with it. She cracked a baby's board-book on a banker, and knocked the hairpiece off a has-been actor with a romance novel. Then the guards frogmarched her outside. She struggled free as a teargas grenade landed at her feet. She bent, picked it up and lobbed it among the fleeing celebs. They screamed and scattered, holding handkerchiefs to their streaming eyes .

Pradip slammed a fist helplessly on the podium. With this public relations disaster, the chances Ramdhun would ever buy his company were slipping away. 'I am doing God's work,' he shouted, ignored by all but Rani.

She laughed. The guards fell back as she wielded a standee support like a spear. News drones swooped over the scene as the cops charged in. In the smoke and chaos, no one saw what dark alleyway swallowed her slim shape. The three girls who were arrested were all children of prominent police and IAS officers. They were out on bail in an hour. Their parents promised to marry them off at the earliest, but the damage, to both Pradip's future and theirs, had been done.

Rimi B. Chatterjee is a novelist, screenwriter and academic based in Kolkata, India. She is the author of *Signal Red* (2005) *The City of Love* (2007) and *Black Light* (2010) as well as an award-winning history of Oxford University Press. Since 2005 she has been working on the Antisense Universe, a parallel future storyworld, in which this story is set. Pradip Shankar is a recurring character from Episode 3 onwards of her TV screenplay Antisense. Recent Antisense works include *Arisudan* (*Mithila Review 15*) and 'Arfabad' in *Multispecies Cities*, an anthology from World Weaver Press. She also teaches English literature at Jadavpur University. More on her work can be found at http://antisenseuniverse.org/.

Bosque Nuboso: Like Someone Humming Against My Palm

Taylor Jones

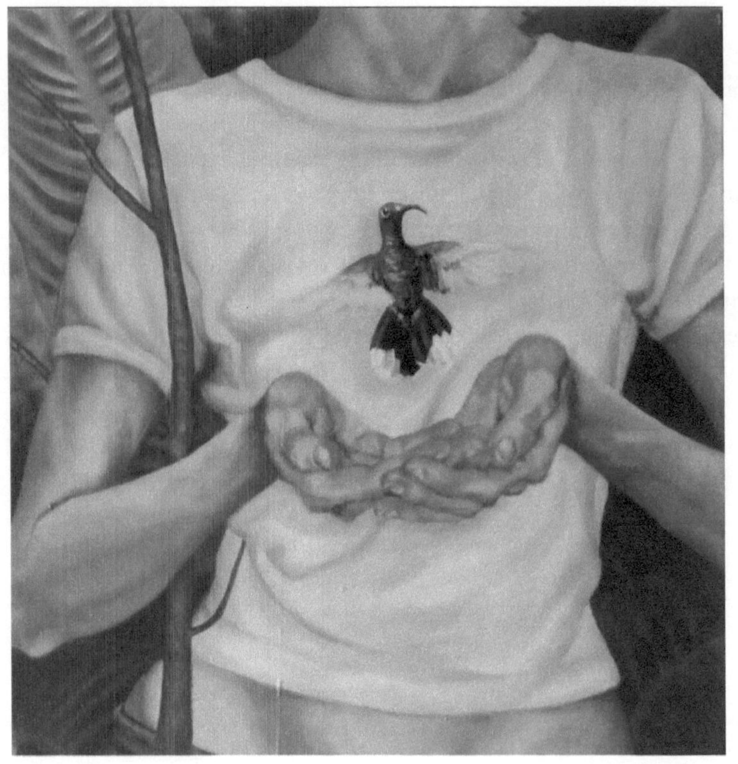

Ghost of a Chance: A Trans Girl Tries to Live

Amber Fox

I am a ghost. I don't know if I was born this way, if I died when I was small, or if it happened later.... For a long time, those questions were important to me. But ghosts like me have existed in every culture and in every age. We existed when acknowledging our existence was punishable by death, we existed even when language didn't have words to describe us. I've come to accept that, and stop my search for answers.

When I was born, the doctor took a cursory look at me and wrote *alive* on my birth certificate, and that was a mistake.

I grew up believing I was alive. My parents, and my brother, were convinced of it. There was no other way for me to be.

I saw ghosts on TV as I grew up. Ghouls who recaptured their bodies and lived in them. Sex workers that were living men's punchlines. That film where the bad guy is a ghost, and he kills living people and skins them, trying to make a body for himself. *It puts the lotion on its skin....* Objects of freak show laughter or terror, written by the living, for the living. About us, but not for us.

So I grew up repulsed by the images of ghosts and ghouls the world gave me to look at. I laughed at them, even if I didn't know why. But the thing about people, about humans, is that we're not meant to exist without bodies. Descartes may have vaingloriously declared *I think, therefore I am*, but he was wrong. Even our language knows it: *Gut instinct*; *heartbroken*; *spineless*; *weak at the knees*. Without body parts, I couldn't feel anything. Just tides pulling me back out to sea. A constant fight for my footing on wet sand as waves pulled at me. I wanted to live, but sometimes, more than anything, I just wanted to stop drowning.

Eventually, I had to turn to face the sea.

I had destroyed everything, fighting it—my partner, my relationship, myself. I'd started standing on the beach but the tide kept coming and now the water was high enough to lap at my chin. It was either turn or drown.

Even then, I didn't know I was a ghost. I had a mountain to climb before I realised the reason I could only feel despair and rage was that I didn't have a body with which to feel anything else. It took me five years to climb. I had no idea what I was doing when I started, no map, no rope, nothing. Sometimes, the only solution is to put on the big girl pants and climb.

It was hard. Dead ends, wrong turns, falls, valleys of shadow and exposed sheer faces. And I had to do it all while still living the life I had fumbled together. Eat, work... well, that's about it, really. I had no friends. Every social interaction held the secret terror of my ghostly nature being discovered. It was still secret even to myself.

Don't try and climb the mountain in one step, I told myself whenever I paused for breath.

Well, I got to the top. I thought I'd find salvation there. You know, hope. Friends. Love. Acceptance. All that good stuff humans need to survive.

What I saw instead was a different version of me. One with rosy cheeks, an easy smile, light dancing in her eyes. "You're a ghost," she said.

"What?"

I looked down at my translucent hands, at my empty chest, my legs drifting like bedsheets, and suddenly felt the yawning tide inside myself. Felt it pulling at me. Silencing and drowning me.

She was right.

I am a ghost.

I'll admit, I fought against it. After all, I wasn't a sex worker or a serial killer skinning people to make a body for myself. I was "normal."

Wasn't I?

No.

And when I recognised that truth it felt almost like I could breathe.

So, I turned to the rosy-cheeked version of me and asked, "What now?"

Nothing but a deafening silence.

I wailed and I wandered. Alone and scared, I stumbled into a hidden valley, and at the end of a dark cave full of pitfalls and monsters I found a pair of doors carved out of shame. My doors.

I pushed them open and stepped in.

I knew my body was in the world, somewhere. Some small shard of divinity had manifested and told me, and I'd learned to listen while climbing that mountain. I couldn't imagine being the bright shining creature from my visitation, but I could at least get out of the water. Feel something other than the constant tide dragging me out to oblivion. If I found my body, I could do that. I could *feel something*.

But when I stepped onto the trailhead beyond the doors, someone blocked the way. They didn't notice me. Their face was a changing smudge above a suit that cost more than I make in a year. A rosette pinned to their chest shifted colours, and their podium sagged under dirty flags and microphones. They dwarfed me and, back turned, they leered into a pit below the podium. Down there, a forest burned. Tinder-dry bracken and a cultivated field browned under drought. Wicked flames and thick, smothering smoke. Famine. People cried out for help. The politician above them called out, "Vote for me and pay no attention to the flames!"

"The *real* problem," they said, still blocking my way, "isn't the fire but the ghosts. If we admit that they're people, then what are you? If they're *not* dead, how can you be alive? *They want to destroy you.*"

Most people were too busy fighting fires or praying for rain for their dusty fields to care. They wanted someone to put out the flames. They wanted to eat. But without the crises, no one would ask the politician for help. So they'd been turning a blind eye and obfuscating while disasters built for decades. The more desperate people are, the more they're willing to give up. That's just basic economics.

"We're going to change the law," the politician said. "No more ghosts. No more ghouls. We'll close the loopholes and strangle them so tight in laws that they won't be able to exist."

Some people cheered. Enough to make me scared. What had I done? Why me? After all I'd done to accept who and what I was, why was I the villain? Maybe, like Dylan said, I was only a pawn in their game.

Some people picked up flaming briars and tossed them onto green patches of ground, warming their hands as the flames caught. Others patted them proudly on the back. Still others watched in horror.

"Excuse me," I said. "Excuse me. Excuse me. *Excuse me.* Excuse me...."

Eventually the politician turned and glanced down at me.

"I want my body back," I said. I saw their lip curl in disgust. Maybe because I'd admitted I was a ghost. Maybe because I wasn't rich like them. Maybe just because I had the audacity to talk to them.

"You'll have to go around," they said.

"But why can't I—"

But they'd already turned back to the flaming forest in the pit. To the spreading drought outside it.

"If we talk to them, it'll be the END of ALL that we are!" they called.

Some people cheered. Others screamed when the fire touched them. Someone threw a flaming log at me, then turned and boasted about what they'd done. A small group emerged from the flames, fleeing for their lives. They were set upon and beaten, the politician urging them on. The crowd turned to look at me and I hurried away, scared of the same fate.

It took a lot of searching to find a way around, but eventually I found a small door surrounded by workmen drilling and cutting and hammering, making it smaller. I joined the back of the line.

It was a very long line.

I'd never noticed the pain before.

It's painful to be a ghost. A spirit *yearns* for a body. Like a body yearns to move its foot from under an anvil. I'd been so convinced I was alive, and so numb, that I'd never noticed my own suffering before. It had still been there, though. That constant being-dragged-out-to-sea feeling. But now for the first time in my life I knew who I was. And the more clearly I knew, the more I wanted my own body.

I'd never felt like I'd belonged with my family, and now I knew why. I'd been a ghost! I ducked out of line and ran excitedly to tell them. Finally, I could have the relationship with them that they thought they had with me. Seeing them wouldn't fill me with anxiety. It wouldn't feel like I was suffocating in the house where I grew up. Their mantras had always been: *nothing is more important than family* and *we just want you to be happy* and *to thine own self be true*. I could skip some of the line if I could cut through my old childhood home.

So, shitting bricks, I pushed open the door, walked inside, and told them.

"These are the things that bring me joy. I'm working on myself, on feeling better, on being happy and fulfilled. It would really help me if you would call me by my living name and treat me like I'm alive. That would really help. I want to be happy."

"You're pretending to be something you're not," my father said. Just as simple as that. "Stop all this, you already *have* a body. We made it for you, now stop taking it away from us."

Shocked, shaking, stunned, I slowly backed away. The door remained ajar, my father's words echoing in my ears. Echoing through the empty vessel I inhabited.

"What about *us*?" he called through the open door. "How about some familial loyalty?"

Slowly, I reached out and pulled the door shut.

I stumbled numbly back to the line.

As I stood in line, waiting, I listened to his voice echoing through me.

I recognised that voice. I knew it. The sound of waves washing up against the shore. The waves that had been trying to drown me my whole life.

I was very quiet, sitting with that realisation. Empty from the mass of it.

"I think I'm a ghost," I told my doctor.

My hands and knees were still bruised from crawling through the tiny door. Covered in mud. My cheeks tear-stained from waiting. And the pain, like living under a jackhammer.

"A what?" the doctor asked. His unfocused eyes lingered in my general direction.

"A ghost," I said. "I need my body."

"Huh," he said, as if he'd read about that somewhere but wasn't paying attention.

"I need a piece of paper from you," I said. He fiddled with something on his desk. "There's another fucking queue I need to join, and I need that piece of paper before they'll let me."

"What… what piece of paper?" he asked, eyes sliding back off into the corner.

I'd talked to the other ghosts in the queue and I knew exactly what form I needed, what he needed to write on it, and where he needed to write it.

Perhaps for some people, being themselves is intuitive. You just wake up in the morning, expel the night gasses, pick up your phone and there you are. Being yourself. Some ghosts get that. Very, very few. It requires so many things to fall into place that the chances are vanishingly small. The rest of us fumble and fight and fuck up, making random movements and listening to the pain, seeing what makes it smaller. There's solidarity in suffering, in fighting the same battles and feeling the same pain. For someone so habitually shy and scared, I was almost gregarious in the line.

So I took a deep breath, put on my big girl pants, and told the doctor exactly what he needed to do and how he needed to do it. He grumbled the whole time and gave me a look I had become familiar with. Suspicious and tired, as if my very existence was both a threat and an annoyance.

But I got my piece of paper. I got to join the second queue. I crawled through the second tiny, narrow door and into another doctor's waiting room. He called me in.

This was a ghost doctor, a doctor for ghosts. He would be on my side.

"So, you think you're a ghost?" he asked.

I nodded.

"Okay, well, convince me," he said. He leaned back and watched me carefully.

This wasn't unexpected. But the problem was, there is an accepted idea of how a ghost should be. What they should have experienced, what feelings they should have felt, what they should have done to try and feel alive. If serial killers were the story of bad ghosts, by the time I got to that second office, there was a story of good ghosts, too.

And my story wasn't the story of a good ghost. I hadn't done any of the things a 'real' ghost had. I hadn't *always known*. I'd just always hurt.

Seeing me a little lost, he threw me a bone.

"What I really want you to do," he said, "is relive all of your past traumas about being a ghost."

So I sat in his office and did just that.

With each word, the door to my pain creaked open further. I walked out deafened from the noise of it. But I had the piece of paper I needed to join the next queue.

The world was changing, and I was, too. When I was young, we put the fire out. It threatened to consume us all, so we gathered together in one long line of humanity, passing buckets from one set of hands to another until the burning pit was gone. I sang a song about it in school assembly. But now I stood in line and watched the fire spread, creeping out from the pit and closing in on everyone. When we pointed to it, the politician turned and pointed to… me. "They are aberrations! Unclean! They mean you harm and anything they say is poison. How can truth come from a mouth so monstrous?"

There was smoke everywhere, but I had my own things to worry about.

I still enjoyed talking to the other people in the line. Still got a sense of community, of solidarity, of not suffering alone. There were even people who had done their time in the lines, and were alive and living, and came back to talk and help and love. It was beautiful.

It didn't last.

Other people came and stood near us. They were alive, and didn't understand who we were, what we wanted, what we were about. They wanted to "understand". So many of us had spent so long not understanding, ourselves, that we were happy to talk.

"But you're dead," they said, cutting us off.

"No, no we're not dead—"

"You're either alive or dead," they said. "You can't be somewhere in between. That's just science."

Some of us were scientists, and tried to explain that according to science the messy business of being alive is far too complicated to fit into binaries.

"Corrupted," the others said. "Captured by the ghosts and forced to speak their words."

"No, no," we said together. "We don't even have any clear clinical definition of being alive and dead—"

"I learnt what it was when I was four," they said. "I *know* what it is."

Behind them, I heard whispers. *Cling to the world you knew when you were too young to know better.*

We tried to tell them the world was a different place to the one they knew as children. That's when the shoving started. And, when no one stopped them, the fists. And, when no one stopped them, the hobnailed boots. And, when no one stopped them, the bats and clubs.

I retreated back inside myself, became shy and silent again. I stood quietly in line and tried not to be noticed.

I got through the second door. Bruised, scratched, bloody. I had to take my voice out of the small box I'd locked it in. This doctor, this one would understand.

"I understand, I understand," he said. "Hmm. Mhmm. Mhmm."

I looked out the window. Even on a perfect day, so many contrails criss-crossed the sky above me. I wondered if I was being selfish. The world was burning and here I was, consumed by my own pain. I told myself that only compassion could save the world and I must start with myself.

I'm not sure I believed it. But I had to try.

"Yes," the doctor said. "Yes, of course. Well, what I need is for you to convince me you're a ghost. If you could just relive your trauma for me...."

Another piece of paper. Another queue.

The beatings continued, and they were different now.

They're pack hunters, these people with their bats and clubs and boots. When one got tired, another took over, and we remained—beaten and beaten and beaten.

I don't want to tell these people why they do what they do. But it's not for survival. We just wanted them to leave us alone. But they hunted us all the same.

"They're stealing children!" oversized shadows yelled, long fingers curling into cones to amplify their voices. "They're an evil octopus, their sticky tendrils are in every organisation. Doctors, lawyers, schools, charities, banks. There's a secret cabal of ghosts controlling everything. Indoctrinating people. Destroying *you*."

Flames leapt up in their footprints.

They're familiar, those words, those accusations. Hauntingly so.

And we tried to point it out, we tried to tell them that this was not the first time those words have been used to hurt people. We told them where it had led last time. But our voices were weak and tired. And the yelling was so very loud.

Over it all, the politicians continued shouting. “Cling to the world you knew when you were four!” they bellowed. “There is no fire! There are no flames, there’s no hunger. You’re hurting because of *them*.”

Seeing a way out, some crawled from the pit and joined the hunting packs. They were given money and attention and validation and love, just so long as they chased and mauled. “We must not let them take their bodies!” the looming shadows called. “It’ll be the end, the end of everything. They’re rapists, and they want to look like you, so you’re easier to hunt. They’ll kill you and take your skin to make a body for themselves. Look at them, *look at them*. How can you trust them?”

Soon, other voices joined in. Voices I’d always trusted to tell me the truth. They lied, and they had no interest in the truth or what we had to say for ourselves. Their voices filled the newspaper stands, the television, the Internet. The politician, seeing their opportunity, sloped over and learned those lines, learned how to repeat them.

“They are the only fire!” they howled, pointing at us.

I watched from the windows of another doctor’s office, not surprised when he said, “I need you to convince me, to relive your trauma. This will be the last time, I promise.”

I reached the top of the mountain three and a half years ago. Forty-two long months. It’s a long time to wait, when salvation is only just beyond your fingertips.

For a long time, society protected us. When the clubs came out and the beatings began in earnest, some protested. Demanded that they leave us alone. Then we appealed to higher powers to *make* them stop.

But the higher powers just shrugged their shoulders and turned away, disinterested.

Next, we tried to take the clubs away. And the people who wielded them had called on those same powers to get them back.

“You realise this is irreversible?” the doctor asked.

“Yeah,” I said, irritated. “That’s the point.”

“And it may not be the answer you’re looking for?”

"Look," I said. "I've lived with this my whole life. Every time I've taken a step down this path, there is less pain. So, I'm going to keep walking it. I want the pain to stop now. It's, it's so bad I can't even think. I *need* it to stop."

I'd been warned about sounding too desperate. If the doctor thinks that you're suffering, they'll deny you your body. For your own good.

"The ghost pain," I said, quickly clarifying. This was a lie, but by now I was so accustomed to saying the untrue, the *expected* thing, that I didn't even notice. "The pain of being non-corporeal, you know? Not being able to pick anything up, not being able to feel anything. I'm lonely and I need to connect with people. I need to open up, stop being this tiny slither of something. I can't open up when I've got nothing to open up with, right? So, I need my body. So I can feel things."

He looked at me over his glasses.

Outside the window, the judge banged his gavel. The packs could keep beating us. They could use their fists and feet and clubs. But nothing metal. No bricks. Wooden clubs were okay.

The doctor gave me my last piece of paper.

The day after my forty-second birthday, I woke up in a hospital bed and took my first breath. I'd never dreamed breathing could feel like this.

It is a bloody and brutal operation to squeeze a ghost back into their body. I was on a morphine pump for the pain and I couldn't move. I dozed, drifting between sleep and wakefulness, a well-meaning nurse waking me every hour to check on me.

I spent that first night being fully human, amazed at the depth of what I could feel. The whole human experience suddenly opened up to me for the first time in my life.

That was almost five months ago, and I'm still getting used to being alive.

The hate is louder than ever and only getting louder. Everybody thinks they own my body. Everybody thinks they have more right to it than me. And the burning world is getting hotter and hotter, so they have to shout louder and louder to distract themselves from that.

But, for the first time in my life, I can fill my fleshy lungs with air, with enough air to breathe and tell them, *No. This body is mine.*

This life is mine. This time on our vanishingly improbable, tiny speck of light, floating in a vast, dark universe is mine.

This body is mine.

Amber Fox is a trans woman living in North Wales. She started her social transition in 2018, around the same time the government began to adopt anti-trans rhetoric and transphobia began to regularly appear in the mainstream media. She graduated with a 2:1 (hons) in English with Creative Writing from the University of Bangor in 2002 and has been writing regularly ever since. She now works for the NHS and as a content writer for Dungeon Studios, who produce own-world content for use with the Dungeons & Dragon RPG system.

Roses in Washington Square Park

Juliana Roth

I sit with my mother across piles of roses, stems clipped
and lined straight in three rows, intersecting. Some chalked

anarchy symbols, others uterus reclaiming. We don't know
where the roses come from, but nobody will pick them up,

then a few do. *Put them back*, a trance over the buds.
A communal understanding not to touch. I look for the artist

as my mother translates what the German men next to us say
over sips of gin. Something about going to Astoria

for a club. One guy likes a blond girl he danced with. *I'm going
to stop now*, my mother whispers. She googles: roses in

Washington Square park. They're like thirty five a dozen,
she repeats. The cost is always considered. I wonder

about the magic of a community of strangers
not touching what isn't theirs.

Juliana was selected as a VIDA Fellow with the Sundress Academy for the Arts for her fiction. Her writing appears in *The Breakwater Review*, *Your Magic*, *Irish Pages*, *Los Angeles Review of Books* as well as being produced as independent films that she directs. Her web series, The University, was nominated by the International Academy of Web Television for Best Drama Writing and screened at survivor justice nonprofits across the country. She writes the weekly newsletter Drawing Animals which features essays, interviews, and doodles celebrating our interconnection with animal life, and teaches writing at NYU.

Green Leaves Against the Wind

Mari Ness

They die in the heat, sometimes. They
die in the afternoon sun, they die
beneath the moon. They need
more water, more shade. They
need—
I could feed this garden
with my blood.
It is hard to breathe, sometimes. Weights
press against my chest. I dig
my fingers into the shallow dust
to make room for something green.
Or hold my blood
within my skin
They die in the cold, sometimes. They
die beneath the shining stars. They die
in the dry air, fading green—
Savoring each precious drop.
Something trembles in the earth.
Something shifts beneath my skin.
And feel
My choices, held tightly
in my pulsing hands
the earth stir beneath my fingertips
as green leaves dance against the wind.

Other work by Mari Ness appears in Tor.com, *Clarkesworld, Uncanny, Lightspeed, Nightmare, Apex, Nature Futures, Diabolical Plots, Kaleidotrope, Strange Horizons, Daily Science Fiction*, and other zines. A poetry novella, *Through Immortal Shadows Singing*, is available from Papaveria Press, and a poetry chapbook, *A Few Mythic Paths*, from Porkbelly Press. For more, check marikness.wordpress.com, or Twitter at @mari_ness. All work is supervised, if not entirely approved, by two magnificent cats.

Hangs Heavy On Their Head

Riley Tao

Later I am a woven mat, to clean oil spills in the Indian Ocean. Before I was a forbidden braid, made with trembling hands and YouTube videos in a locked and midnight bathroom. But now I am loose and free, lax between the stylist's comb and humming shears, as Lian meets their own eyes in the wall-length mirror.

"Just the left side," they say.

The stylist winks. "I hear you," he says.

And then he begins to trim.

It is nothing like when Lian first shaves themself. They don't dare buy shaving cream. A razor could be slipped into a hoodie's sleeve. A can of liquid could not. Instead they rub shampoo into their warm-soaked legs, like they do to me and my hundred thousand siblings on the occasions they could force themself to strip and shower and see themself, all of themself, even the parts they wish they could take a blade to and make disappear, like how with each pass of the razor the jungle sprouting from their skin thins and thins and thins. Until their skin is smooth and bare as farmland. They watch their hairs swirl down the drain and ask whose nightmares they are now. And I know that their body is theirs alone, its terrors only for them to see.

Then, they are lying in bed and watching Australia burn in the palm of their hand. They wonder if the world would heal faster without them in it. Their father throws open the door. He holds up a mass of tangled hairs in one hand, a plunger in the other.

"You can't pass your classes, but you can waste your time and my money on vanity?" Lian flinches as their father hurls the evidence of their crimes in their face, and the tangled hairs are thick with sewage. "How dare you?"

Lian mumbles an apology, they're sorry for hurting him, they didn't mean to, they'll clean up their mess, and their father isn't there anymore, and Lian runs a thumb along my side, numbly, and I am greasy and tangled from weeks without washing, and if I had any more oil America would invade. Lian's legs are prickly, they hurt them with every step, but as long as they eat their father's food and sleep under their father's roof, they daren't hurt him by shaving again.

The stylist's blade scythes through me, and I am free, dancing around Lian's shoulders as I arc to the ground. Lian's father is not here.

Lian's father is years and miles and memories away. But still he scoffs as the stylist's nimble fingers work. "Twenty dollars for a sideshave? I could do that myself." His eyes track each drifting hair as if he could count their costs. As if he could see the entirety of time from behind every eye, weigh the agonies and blessings of any choice, and with the confidence of eternity deem Lian's haircut an injustice.

And Lian is filthy, scrubbing furiously at their tangled hair, feeling the muck of months wash free from their skin. Lian's father is outside the bathroom door. Lian takes short showers. He appreciates that about them. Lian shakes the water from their hair, feeling the pleasant, soaked weight of it. Their hair could hold so much, they think. More than its weight in water. They wonder what else it could hold.

I land at Lian's feet, and the stylist steps back. One half of Lian's hair pours over their shoulder like black gold. The other is bare, stark, controlled, theirs. Very little is theirs, nowadays. A room they share, a job they hold, a form they own. Even their ideas are not their own. They wonder—if hair can cling to so much oil in water, could it perhaps soak oil from the dark-spilled seas? They search the Internet and are not sure whether to be disappointed that they are not the first, that a company in San Francisco has been making oil nets from human hair since before Lian knew their name.

I have known it all along, that Lian is neither the beginning nor the end. My long strands are swept aside, and Lian regards themself, the sleek and shimmer of their hair, while the stylist counts up the price.

Lian's father is not here, but he spits, "Was it *worth* it? For you to *feel* better?"

Nobody is there to respond, but Lian's lips still quirk up as they say, "Let's find out."

Later, I am a woven mat, to clean oil spills in the Indian ocean. Before, I was a forbidden braid, made with trembling hands and YouTube videos in a locked and midnight bathroom. But now I am proud as Lian rises, thanks the stylist, and lives the strand of their life to its nowless end.

Riley Tao (they/them) is a Californian college student who has been rejected by eighty-five literary agents while seeking representation for their YA fantasy novel, who turned to writing short stories after deciding that maybe they should walk before they run. They spent six months updating a creative writing blog with short stories on a weekly basis at rileyriles.wordpress.com before deciding to focus on a second novel. They also love computer science and mathematics, and in their free time they play homebrewed RPGs and hug their cat.

Bosque Nuboso: Nocturne

Taylor Jones

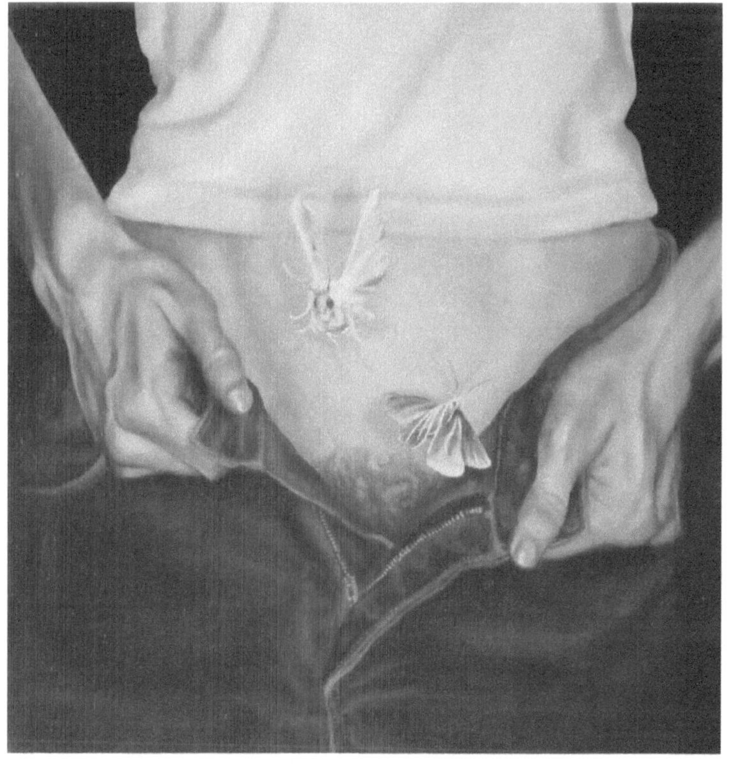

Taylor Jones' fiction, poetry, and art is inspired by her background in and love of biology. Her writing has appeared in *Spit Poet Zine*, *Smoky Quartz*, *South Broadway Ghost Society*, *Barren Magazine*, and *Reckoning*. Her work can be found here: linktr.ee/i_heart_fungi. She was born and raised on the East Coast, but now lives in Denver, Colorado, in a house full of plants.

Those Dark Halls

M.C. Benner Dixon

Paige was twelve years old when she first noticed the buds along her spine. She was in the upstairs bathroom, the one with the vining yellow flowers in the wallpaper and the faux-tile linoleum, about to get in the shower. She stopped to examine herself in the mirror above the sink, not yet steamed with the hot water. Did her elbows look weird? Were her widening hips and thighs fat or beautiful? She turned and twisted, trying to see herself from every angle. Pulling her long, pecan-colored hair forward over her shoulder, she noticed the little constellation of four raised bumps in the middle of her back, two on each side of her spine, just between her shoulder blades. Her stomach jolted.

She knew what they were, of course. Sort of knew. Her mother had spoken of her own chambers abstractly: a promise, an honor, a gift from God. But seeing those bumps there on her own back, raised up under her own skin—as yet, the color of the rest of her and featureless—Paige did not feel honored at all. What right did God have to put chambers into *her* back? It would be years still until the buds would split open, a pouch having formed inside each one, and the tenant moths would come to lay their eggs in the little hollow chambers. But in her horror, Paige thought she could feel the moth larvae in there already, moving and growing, taking possession of her in their small way.

Paige didn't tell her mom about the chambers after she discovered them that day in the bathroom mirror. Instead, she got into the shower and tried to scrub them off until her arms ached. She didn't want to be a keeper. If this was a blessing, then she didn't want blessings. Paige saw the faces that people made at her mother's exposed back during tenant season, heard them grumbling at her, telling her to cover up. Not everyone was rude. Most people didn't care. But there were always a few who wanted to talk about it. If their parents had friends over for dinner in the summer, they might do a special toast to the moths and to Paige's mother. And then they would ask about the girls with curiosity.

"Not yet," their mom would say, looking wistfully at her daughters. "Lord willing."

Every year, on their anniversary, their dad made the same joke:

"She's a keeper," he always said, and his eyes crinkled up as he looked at their mom, "in more ways than one."

Paige didn't want any of this said about her. She thought that if she didn't tell her mother, it wouldn't happen. So she told her sister instead.

Heather was fifteen, a young-for-her-grade sophomore, who nonetheless was a favorite among the juniors and seniors. She seemed, to Paige, to know all the secrets of fitting in and had taught Paige everything she knew about fashion, make-up, and sleepover etiquette. And so, body wrapped in a large green towel, hair turbaned into a pink one, and eyes red from shampoo and crying, Paige crept into Heather's room.

"What, Paigelina?" Heather was belly-down on her bed, reading a novel, her chin propped on the heel of her hand. "I'm busy."

"Can I tell you something? But you can't tell mom."

"What is it?"

"You can't tell mom, though."

Heather put her finger in her book and looked at Paige. "I won't. What is it?"

Paige turned around and lowered the towel a little.

"Paige. What are you—" And then Heather was quiet. Paige turned her head over her shoulder to look at her sister's hard, blank face.

"They're just zits, right?" Paige begged her sister. Heather got up and walked closer, tossing her book onto her pillow.

"I don't think so."

"Can you just try and pop them?"

"Ew, no."

"Please, Heather? Please? I don't want them." Paige felt the tears rising in her eyes again.

Behind her, Heather made a sound of annoyance—a grating in the back of her throat. "Fine." She put a finger on each side and squeezed the buds until her fingernails left bright red marks on Paige's skin. Paige bit her lip and whimpered. When Heather finally gave up, Paige threw herself onto Heather's bed and cried into the lilac-print comforter. Heather sat beside her, petting her little sister's calves gently. Eventually, Heather took a breath as if to speak but sighed it out. She put her hand back in her lap and tried again.

"It's probably too late for me, right?"

"What do you mean?" Paige asked, wiggling her way into a sitting position, clinging to her towel.

"It's just, you're younger than me, so if you're getting them now, I won't, right?"

"How would I know?"

"Sometimes people don't show until they're older, but it's probably too late for me. I think that's how it works."

"Do you want them?" Paige could hardly believe this. Heather showed no interest whatsoever as their mom tracked her tenancies in her little red journal or asked for someone to help her dab cream on the skin around the chambers. Paige hadn't been interested either, and she wasn't interested now.

Heather didn't speak right away. She looked into Paige's teary eyes, then away. "Of course I don't want them. No one wants them." Paige felt, in these words, a cruel new reality settling over her: she was something different from her sister, now.

Both Heather and their mother denied that Heather had told, but it was only two days later when, under the pretense of tucking a tag back into Paige's shirt, their mother saw the still-bruised buds and gave a little yelp of joy, covering her mouth with her hands. Almost in a single breath, she scolded Paige for the bruises and began telling her what a gift it was. She couldn't stop touching the emergent chambers. She let go of Paige only long enough to disappear upstairs. She came back with a little book that she had stashed away in her dresser, just in case: *Tenant Moths and You, a Guide for Keepers.* She handed it over as if it were a diploma.

That night at dinner, as they all held hands, her mother added a special prayer to the meal's blessing:

"And Lord," she had said, her voice unsteady with emotion, "I just want to thank you for making your will known in the life of our Paigey. We thank you for making her a part of your plan for this world and for revealing to her and to us all this one small part of her mission here on Earth. We bless your name and thank you for your mercy. In Jesus' name, Amen."

Paige did not say "Amen" with the others. The buds in her back felt sore and massive, like heavy stones. Whatever she did now, she did it as a keeper. From now on, for the rest of her life. She would be a keeper doctor, a keeper teacher, a keeper beautician. God had decided for her. Without even asking. Without caring what she wanted.

It took five years for the buds to darken, thicken, and open. Another five for the skin inside to fully mature and the top fold to extend down like an eyelid over the bottom, signaling readiness.

The drive to her parents' house was just over an hour—far enough to justify living on campus but not far enough that Paige could get out of regular family dinners with her parents and Heather, who still lived close.

The smell of tuna casserole and cooked peas hit Paige as soon as she came through the door. She tossed her keys into her backpack and called her hello into the empty front rooms. The table in the dining room was set, a pitcher of ice water making a little damp spot on the tablecloth. Paige threw her backpack into the corner of the living room beside Heather's angular peach-and-white purse.

Paige's mother came bustling out of the kitchen to greet her daughter.

"Oh, honey, you look a mess." There was concern in her voice.

"Thanks, mom."

"Is that Paigelina?" It was Heather, still in the kitchen. "You're late."

"I know, shut up. I was working on that big stats project." She had spent hours trying to make sense of the sample data, but anytime she reached for the words to explain how the data's underlying probability distribution might intersect with her claims that checklist protocols could reduce racial disparity in home visits, certainty slipped away from her. "I wish I could drop the class, but it's a requirement for my program."

"I'm sorry, honey," their mother said. "Are you hungry? We waited dinner for you."

"Yeah, I am. Thanks. Sorry I'm late."

Paige's mother turned back towards the dining room. "Heather, can you call Dad? Tell him we're ready."

Heather breezed through the dining room and over to the stairs, booping Paige's nose on the way by. She bounded up in a few long-legged strides to find their father.

Paige didn't have much to add to the conversation at dinner, but it didn't matter. Heather filled the air with stories. She had just gotten back from her friend Kari's bachelorette party in Costa Rica. Paige listened reflexively, imagining her sister ziplining through the jungle like some well-preened travel brochure model, impossibly spruce in all that humidity. Would it have been different, Paige wondered as she rolled her peas around on her plate, if Heather were the keeper instead of her? Would she fly so blithely through the canopy if she was? Heather had always been concerned about her "image," saving every dollar for an eyeshadow palette or the exact right pair of jeans. Even when she was drunk, she was pretty. Even when she was sleeping. It was annoying.

"How's that stats project coming?" their dad asked, trying to give Paige a chance to talk, but Paige didn't particularly want it.

She shrugged and got up to clear her plate. "It's okay. It's hard, but I think I'll pass the class."

"I should take a stats class," Heather said, sitting back and letting her mother take her plate. She tapped thoughtfully at her chin. "It would look good on my resume. There's a senior brand management position opening up, and I'm going to go for it." The conversation veered back to Heather, and Paige wandered to the living room, picking up a year-old copy of National Geographic from the coffee table.

She was flipping through a photo essay on prairies when their mother came out to the living room, wiping her hands on her hips and pausing at the bottom of the staircase. "Paigey, can you come upstairs with me? There are some boxes I want you to look through." Paige's old bedroom was slated to become a craft room, and her mom had been on a cleaning spree to make space for all the hot glue guns, glass beads, shears, and rolls of fabric that she had been stuffing in a hallway closet for years. Paige got to her feet and followed obediently up the stairs.

"I'm thinking of a murphy bed," Paige's mother said as she slid a dilapidated banker's box out from under the desk, "so I can spread out when no one's sleeping here."

"You could've just thrown these away," Paige said, leafing through high school history papers and chemistry tests piled in the worn cardboard box.

"There might be something in there that you still want," her mom said. She pulled the heavy curtains back from the window with both hands and tilted her head to consider them.

"What could I possibly want?" There was a certificate of participation for band. A playbill from the one musical she had participated in her sophomore year. Junk.

Then Paige understood. She opened a blue-grey folder and flipped through the handouts, charts, and pamphlets inside. It was everything that she had acquired over the years in her keeper classes. She became aware that her mother had turned from the window and was watching her. "Mom, I don't need any of this stuff," she said without looking up.

"Oh, but you don't know how you're going to feel your first time, dear. It'll be so nice to have some information handy. Just hang onto it."

Paige sighed and closed the folder. She dropped the other papers back on top of the keeper materials and turned to face her mother. "Really, I don't need it."

"Well, I'm just going to hang onto it for you." Her mom took the banker's box from her and set it on top of Paige's old desk.

"It's your house. Keep whatever you want."

They were quiet for a moment. Paige looked around the room. She had spent a lot of time up here, hiding from the world.

"Paigey," her mom said. Paige knew what was coming. "Can I do a little check? Would you mind?"

Paige sighed again. "Sure." She sat down on the desk chair and hitched her shirt up over her shoulders, giving her mother a clear view of her back. Paige knew what her mother was seeing. It wasn't like she hadn't been checking them herself.

"Soon, now," Paige's mother told her, touching the chambers, gently prodding and inspecting.

"Yeah, maybe. Who knows?" Paige shrugged at her shirt and shifted on the chair, uncomfortable with the attention.

"Don't worry, honey." Her mother's voice sounded soft and faraway. She tapped lightly on Paige's back. "It will be your turn soon."

Paige hadn't been worried. She didn't resent God anymore for giving her tenant moth chambers. But then, she didn't really believe in God anymore. The chambers, she knew now, were not a divine gift or a punishment—just a recessive genetic attribute. Her mother had both copies of the gene, but her father had never been tested, so until Paige's buds appeared, no one knew if the girls would be keepers like their mother.

Paige had always thought that Heather's life must be, on the whole, simpler because she was not a keeper. She didn't have to think about the someday occupation of her body, learn to sleep on her stomach, go to once-a-month programs with other keeper kids to learn about the reproductive cycle of tenant moths and special hygiene for the chambers. For a long time, Paige had felt sure that Heather was happier than she was because of this.

But somehow, the closer the chambers got to maturity, the less they seemed to matter. Paige had other things to worry about now—legitimate things. As she sat there on the chair, letting her mother coo over her chambers, she still had three final papers to write, not to mention the stats project. She would rather not think about the chambers at all, but there they were. And here her mother was, reminding Paige of them at every opportunity.

"I'm not worried, Mom," she said.

"Of course not, honey. It's all part of God's plan. And it will be very good for you, you know. There are lots of health benefits." Paige knew the studies her mother was referring to; she recited them to her all the time. A mild mood elevation during tenancy, a slight bump in longevity for keepers.

"Hey, you guys—oh, sorry." Heather withdrew immediately from the doorway where she had leaned in, face bright, a moment before.

"What is it, honey?" their mother asked, still touching Paige's back with her cool fingertips.

Heather remained out of sight in the hallway. "Dad wanted me to tell you the brownies were ready, but if you're...."

"It's fine, Heather. We're done," Paige said, shrugging off her mother's touch and pulling her shirt back down. "It's safe."

Paige hadn't planned on being a social worker. She entered undergrad as an elementary education major. Every week when their Introduction to Elementary Education class had an afternoon block, they would all be shuttled around to different schools in the region to get real in-class experience. After a few placements with older grades, which did not interest her, Paige had been put in a first-grade classroom at a small private school. The teacher, Una—everyone went by first names at this school, so she was Una to students and Paige alike—had, at first, seemed like everything Paige wanted to be: kind, creative, intuitive.

Halfway through free-play time, two children started shouting and slapping at each other over by the little plastic kitchen set. Una rushed over, putting herself between them.

"Hey, no! Stop, stop! What happened?" Una asked, her voice sorrowful. She looked at the little boy. "Remy?"

"Jewel won't let me play," Remy complained. "It's not fair."

"Jewel? Everyone's allowed to play with the toys. You know that. What's going on, sweetie?" At first, the little girl was silent, tears falling steadily and her nose dripping. But Una was patient and tender and finally, Jewel started talking, though her voice was so quiet that Paige couldn't hear what she was saying. Una's eyes filled as she listened.

"Remy? Does that help you understand what Jewel was thinking?"

"I'm sorry about your grandma, Jewel," Remy said. And his own chin crinkled with tears. "Do you want a hug?" Jewel nodded, her eyes on the ground. Remy squeezed her in his arms and let go, and Jewel dissolved into sobs. Una picked her up and carried her into the hallway.

Later in the afternoon, Paige went outside with the kids for recess and watched them swarming over the playground. The air was thick with their laughter. The chains of the swingset chimed against the steel pole, and the spring riders were alive with gleeful motion. This is good, Paige thought. This is what kids need. But then, behind Paige, came a sneering little voice:

"Keeper, keeper, booty-peeper!"

Paige stiffened, her stomach clenching. Her hand went to her neckline to see if it had slipped down to expose the bumps on her back. But as she turned, she realized that the child was not taunting her but a classmate, a little boy with big glasses.

"Your mama's a keeper, your daddy's a keeper, your dog is a keeper, your fish is a keeper...."

"No they aren't. Animals aren't," the boy whined in response to his tormentor.

"Yours are! And you're gonna be a keeper, too!"

"I'm not!" The little boy was growing panicked, breathing harder.

"You are," said one of the other kids gathered around him. "If your mommy *and* your daddy are, then you are."

"Moths are going to mess up your brain! You're going to be a zombie."

"That's not true!"

"It is true. I know. My dad's a scientist, and he said keepers are...."

Paige turned fully towards the group and took a step in their direction. The ringleader, a chinless kid with flat, stone-brown hair, glanced up at her, then elbowed the others.

"Just kidding," said the chinless kid through a gappy grin. "We're just joking, Ry." And Ry was treated to a round of excuses, each of the bullies shooting a look up at Paige before they peeled off.

"You okay, Ry?" Paige asked.

"Uh-huh," Ry said, trying to keep it together. "It was just a joke."

"It wasn't a very funny joke, though, was it?"

Ry dropped his head. "Does it mess up your brain?"

"No, sweetheart," Paige said, crouching down. "Nothing happens to your brain." Paige wasn't actually sure about this. She had more or less stopped reading the articles her mother sent her. "But did you know that keepers actually have a slightly longer life expectancy?"

Ry stared at her.

"That means keepers live longer than other people."

"They do?"

"Yeah, buddy. Don't listen to those kids. Being a keeper is no big deal."

"Have you done it?" Ry asked, his eyes drifting towards her shoulder.

Paige shook her head. "But my mom is a keeper. She's hosted lots of times, and she's definitely not a zombie." She smiled at Ry and sent him back to play.

At their debriefing at the end of the day, Paige told Una about the playground. Una tsked her tongue and swept her curly, dark hair back from her face.

"Oh, poor Ry. Why do we wait so long to educate kids about… about the moths?" She flitted her long-fingered hands in the air. "We really should start introducing these things earlier. And not just for the ones who…." She waved her hands back over her own shoulders. "I mean, keepers aren't some kind of Other. Kids need to hear that message while they're young, before it's clear who's who. Keepers don't even know for sure until they're, what? Ten?"

"Sometimes older," Paige said. Una's enthusiasm made her uncomfortable. "You want to do a lesson?"

"Yeah, you know—about the eggs and the moth season." Una's voice was lively with excitement. "Gosh, just talking about this is making me realize: all of us really need this. It's not like anyone taught *us* about them, right?"

Paige smiled tightly, but she did not correct Una's assumption about her. "Totally," she said.

"I love this, Paige. I wonder if Ry's mom or dad would want to come in and talk to our classes."

Paige imagined having her own mother in front of a room of her peers, turning around to show her swollen chambers, red and full with their tenants. "Wouldn't that put Ry in a weird spot?"

Una finished up a note to herself on her phone and brushed away a curl of hair that had fallen across her forehead. "But here's the thing, right? Ry is already in a weird spot. He is *going* to be a keeper, and so he's going to have to deal with that."

"So, if all the kids learn about tenancy...."

Una beamed at Paige. "Right. They can understand the keeper kids. They can help share the burden."

Paige couldn't stop thinking about what Una had said. At dinner, she took her plate of lasagna and wan green beans to an empty table in the dining hall and stared out into the November twilight. The word "burden" bothered her more, somehow, than the playground teasing. From that first night in the bathroom, staring at her back in the mirror, Paige had hated the fact that she was a keeper; as her chambers puckered and deepened year by year in anticipation of their tenants, she had agonized over them, but it wasn't because hosting was a "burden." Keepers barely had to do anything. She had observed her mother's summer tenancies, and they were nothing. A little swelling, a little itching maybe, a little extra attention paid, but not burdensome. The only reason she hated being a keeper was because other people thought it meant something. It didn't. It didn't mean anything.

Una's plan to turn Ry into an object lesson was exactly the wrong approach. Paige knew all too well that the cruelty of playground bullies wasn't a matter of misunderstanding. Tenancy wasn't that complicated. Some people have chambers on their backs. The tenant moth lays its eggs in the chambers. The larvae crawl out when they are ready. Whatever made kids tease other kids about turning into zombies, whatever made Heather recoil whenever the topic came up, it wasn't a lack of information. That impulse was already there, looking to find its way out.

So she withdrew from Intro to Elementary Education and changed her major to Psychology. On the advice of her professors, she applied to a respected graduate social work program, not too far from home. Her acceptance had felt like a sign.

Finals came and went, and Paige pulled in a B- in Stats, acing her social work-specific classes. Summer term would begin in a week. Paige had a practicum lined up with a women's center on the north side of the city. She was only vaguely aware of the news that tenant moths had been spotted in town—a headline from a local news station had popped up in her feed. She didn't even open the article. She just clocked the news and moved on.

She should start paying closer attention. This was probably the year when a tenant moth, having flirted in the dusky evening air with a mate, would find her, alight between her shoulders, and deposit its eggs into one of her chambers. Her mom had bought her a few keeper shirts—some with open backs, some with more discreet slits—but she only wore them when she had her hair down to hide their function. It was customary for keepers to either leave their windows open at night or take evening walks during the breeding weeks. Paige didn't do any of this. If it happened, it happened. A few weeks, and even the small inconveniences of hosting would be over, and her life would return to normal until next summer. *Just a few weeks*, she told herself whenever the thought surfaced. *It's nothing.*

It was a Thursday evening, and Paige was walking through the parking lot of the Shoprite, on her way to get some milk and eggs and a few other odds and ends, when the moth blundered into her face. She jerked away and swatted at the bug, not fully registering its import. Undeterred, the moth returned and landed on her right shoulder. Paige craned her neck to see it. Between the lights of the parking lot and the lingering sunset in the summer sky, Paige could make out its distinguishing features. Dark, fuzzy thorax and striped abdomen, tufted at its end; the wings, a soft, veined grey, with a greenish band edging the forewings and a single, black splotch on each hindwing. All light seemed to disappear into its compound eyes. Paige was surprised to find her heart racing a little. The moth began to crawl, its legs tickling her bare shoulder as it made its way toward her back. Paige gently pulled her hair forward to clear the way.

"Oh my god, look," said a woman walking up behind Paige. Paige was still frozen in place, not knowing if her movement would scare the moth off. Out of the corner of her eye, she could see the woman staring, another figure beside her. The pair of them apparently felt no shame in gawking openly at the spectacle now taking place in and on Paige's body.

"Gross," said the woman, or her companion maybe. Then they kept walking, strolling through the sliding doors of the grocery store with a lingering glance of disgust back at Paige.

Angry and nervous, Paige eased herself towards a bench a few feet from the entrance, its back against the plate glass of the storefront.

Paige sat on the far end of the bench, where she would be shielded by a large vinyl decal advertising pre-made salads and juice smoothies for sale inside. She did not want anyone else to see this. She might be resigned to this tenancy, but she was not resigned to being casually, comfortably reviled by some bitch on her way to get a case of Diet Coke and a twelve-pack of toilet paper.

As she sat and waited, Paige began to calm. She could feel the faint tickle of the moth's fine feet and its tufted abdomen. She remembered practicing this part of the tenancy in keeper classes when she was young: simulating the crawl and ovipositing with paint brushes so that the children could learn to keep still as it happened. Paige sat patiently as the tenant moth did her quiet work.

As she waited, Paige thought about her summer practicum at the women's center, about the women she would meet, drowning in a ruthless system, their abusers hovering in the shadows. Her heart swelled with the desire to protect those women. She cut herself off abruptly—that was savior bullshit, as her Micro Practice professor would call it. And she had to cut it out. Micro Practice was taught by a woman who had been a social worker with the city for twenty-five years.

"You aren't here to save anyone," she said to them. "Get that out of your heads. This is work, not missionary service. Even if you do your job perfectly, you don't save anyone at the end of the day. And you aren't going to do your job perfectly. Make peace with that. You are going to make mistakes and miss things and watch the consequences fall on other people. You do not have the worst end of the deal, here. Your *clients* do. The things that bring your clients to you in the first place—hunger, poverty, mental illness, racism, trauma—they're big-ass problems. You do what you can to help them navigate the system, but you cannot and you will not *save them*. That's not the job. Go in expecting to save people, and you will burn yourself to the ground and take everyone else down with you."

The best she could hope for was to help a little if she could. Paige leaned forward as she had been taught, straightening her shoulders to relax the skin of her back. Maybe she owed this to the universe—giving herself to somebody, even if it was just a soft-bodied moth with light-absorbing eyes. It was a little thing, she reminded herself, such a little thing to be a keeper.

There was the barest flutter by Paige's left ear, and she turned to see the moth fly off. Perhaps to lay additional eggs in another keeper's chamber. Perhaps to die. But the moth had done her work. She had laid her eggs and, on her feet, carried a fungus which would now proliferate in the pouch as the eggs developed. By hatching time, there would be a scaly, yeasty overgrowth all around the eggs. It would discolor Paige's skin, but it would give the larvae their first food. When the caterpillars vacated the chambers, her body would regain its natural balance.

She should probably get the app, Paige thought. She pulled her phone out and went to the app store. Her finger hesitated over the download button. It wasn't strictly necessary. She could track the dates of this clutch of eggs and those that might be laid in her other chambers over the next few weeks manually, like her mother used to. The memory of that little red-backed grid-paper notebook brought with it a tart mix of nostalgia, affection, sadness, and revulsion. She clicked the download button quickly, looking away over the parking lot as the program loaded. When she looked down again, there on her screen was a new little icon of a tenant moth cupped in a pair of hands. Paige's eyes stung and blurred, and she blinked, sending the tears streaming down her face. She felt silly crying about this thing that was so peripheral to her life. She wiped her tears and forced herself to enter her age, weight, height, and gender along with the date and location of the deposit. If she didn't do it right away, she might never open the app again.

After the buds appeared, Paige's mother had started telling stories about Paige's grandpa, who died when she was only four.

"He was so proud of being a keeper," her mom told her as they looked at a picture of him: young, slight-figured and hard-eyed. "He said that when he first developed—and he was even younger than you, Paigey—all the kids at his school envied him. Some even tried to pretend they were keepers. They would catch bees and make them sting their backs to get the welts. Can you imagine that?"

"No," Heather had said. She was in the dining room, working on her homework at the table. "They must have been crazy. It's so gross."

"Heather, stop it. That's unkind," their mother scolded, waving her older daughter back to her schoolwork. "He always said it was the greatest honor of his life. 'The Lord doesn't choose just anyone,' he used to say. He'd be so proud of you, honey."

Paige had nodded, secretly glad that he had never known this about her.

"No one envies keepers anymore, Mom," Heather said.

Their mother had frowned. "Well, they should. It's a very special experience."

It wasn't just the stories, though. Everything in Paige's life seemed to be about the chambers. There were the keeper diet kicks, which her mom heard about from a friend or found online. For months at a time, Paige wouldn't be allowed white flour or sugar. Heather and their dad would be having dinner rolls and corn on the cob with their Sunday roast beef, while Paige suffered through dry slices of sprouted-grain bread and bitter greens in a watery pile.

"Mom, please," Paige would beg, "can I just have normal food?"

"It's good for us, honey," her mother would reply, pulling out the bag of stiff, brown sliced bread from the freezer. "It helps develop the chambers."

"But it's disgusting. And it doesn't even matter. I asked my counselor at the keeper class, and they said keepers can eat anything anyone else can."

"This is good, healthy food, Paigey. We can't let it go to waste." Paige came to dread the sight of grocery bags on the counter, never sure what she would be forced to eat next.

Worst of all were the Saturday morning brunches with her mother's keeper friends. The whole morning would be them complaining about disrespectful comments, about the reduced tax credit, about insulting misconceptions that had ruffled their feathers.

"What we do is a benefit to this world," they would say to one another. "The research has only just begun to reveal the full extent of what God has ordained in us. People forget. These surgeries they're having. It's a sin! To reject a gift that God has given is a sin."

"Remember that, Paigey," her mother would tell her. "You cannot change who you are."

Once, Paige's mother had taken her to the cemetery on their way home from brunch. It was a bright April day, though the sun was layered away behind a film of clouds. Paige stood sullenly beside her mother in the chilly afternoon and looked at her grandfather's gravestone. Above his name, its wings spread wide, was the carved image of a tenant moth. Paige cried when she saw it. That night, she wrote instructions for her own funeral in her journal, forbidding anyone from mentioning moths.

The first day at the women's center consisted mostly of following the director, Irina Poe, from one room to another and being introduced to harried staff as they passed in the hallway. While Irina took a call with a grant officer, Paige worked through the forms on confidentiality and liability. She was left to imagine what sort of dangers, exactly, were implied here, as the language was fairly broad. She signed anyway, as easily as she agreed to the terms and conditions of the keeper app, as easily as she signed her student loan papers, as easily as she had sworn whatever she had sworn when she had been fingerprinted for the background check. Paige wondered how many of these contracts she had violated in her life—sharing a password, checking the wrong box. If all her agreements were enforced, what would her life be? But she was counting on the fact that no one would ever come after her with evidence of her carelessness.

"Did you bring your lunch?" Irina asked. Paige looked up from the clipboard. Irina had finished the call, placed her phone face down on a pile of paper-thick folders, and was now rubbing her eyes and face wearily.

"I didn't," said Paige, flustered. "I wasn't sure if there was a fridge or...."

"You know what?" Irina said. "Why don't I take you to this little place around the corner? Do you like Indian food?"

"Definitely," Paige said, embarrassed by forcing her new supervisor into a position of needing to feed her.

"Great. Let me get my purse." Irina tossed her phone in and fished around until she found a pair of semi-iridescent bug-eye sunglasses and pushed them into her coiffed hair. "Okay, follow me."

Paige did as she was told, grabbing her backpack from the corner of the office, just in case Irina wasn't actually offering to pay for lunch.

On their way to the front door, Irina stopped to let Taja, who coordinated the counseling programs at the center, know that she would be out of the building for about an hour.

"Okay," Taja said. She was sitting at the reception desk, eating salad out of a repurposed takeout container as she flipped through a stack of paperwork. "When you get back, though, can we talk about the intake rooms?"

Irina sighed. "Yes, Taja. We're going to talk about that." Irina looked at Paige with an expression of mixed annoyance and apology.

"Space is a constant issue for us." Paige nodded, unsure of what else Irina wanted from her in response.

The front door swung open, and a woman ushered her slow-footed son—probably ten or eleven years old—out of the bright summer afternoon.

"Well, look who it is," Taja said, a wide smile on her face. "Evan, Evan, Pumpkin Pie." The kid smiled a little, then immediately took a seat in one of the cushy chairs in the lounge. He picked up a home decorating magazine and opened it. Taja laughed and pouted. "Okay, you be that way. It's fine. You're not hurting my feelings."

Irina gave her attention to the mother. "Hello, Mandy. Nice to see you. How are you?"

The woman took off her sunglasses, revealing a bruised and bleeding face. Paige gasped loudly. Irina and Taja both shot her warning looks. Taja put down her fork.

"Mandy," Irina said, readjusting her hold on her purse strap, "do you need me to take you to the hospital?"

The woman, Mandy, moved her head uncertainly. "I don't know." Her voice was raw. "I'm sorry. I just—I don't know."

Irina shook her head. "That's okay, my dear. I do want to see you taken care of, though. Is the hospital okay? Does that feel safe?"

"I don't know," Mandy said.

The phone rang, and Taja answered it, turning away to talk, though Paige saw her eyes darting over to where Evan sat.

"Mandy," Irina was saying, "why don't we go back to my office? You can sit down. You and I can figure out next steps together." Irina extended one hand towards Mandy and the other back down the hallway towards her office. "Is Evan hurt?"

Mandy shook her head, looking at her son sitting on the chair, seemingly absorbed in the magazine. "He didn't touch him."

"Okay," Irina said. "Paige, would you sit with Evan while Mandy and I talk?"

"Sure," Paige said. "Of course."

"Taja will be here if you need anything."

Taja smiled up at Paige, putting her hand over the receiver. "I'll be right over," she whispered.

Irina and Mandy walked back towards Irina's office, and Paige went over to the boy and stood beside his chair.

"Hi, Evan," she said to him. He shifted in his seat, looking over at her dull, office-appropriate shoes. "I'm Paige. Is it okay if I sit beside you?" Her voice sounded strained to her, and she cleared her throat.

"Yeah." Evan turned his eyes back to the page, which was ruffling in the breeze from the open window.

"Thanks." Paige sat down. "I'm just going to sit here with you so that you're not alone. We can talk if you want, but it's okay to be quiet, too."

"Mm-hm," said Evan. Paige wondered how many times he had done this. He had not turned the page of the magazine. Paige paced her own breathing, letting it grow slower and steadier, hoping this would somehow communicate to Evan, intangibly, a sense of calm.

A soft tapping at the open window to Paige's right drew her attention. Evan, too, looked up at the window. A moth with green-edged wings was bumping at the screen. It was unusual for them to be out at this time of day, but perhaps this one had been weathering the brightness under the windowsill and was tempted into the light by Paige's pheromones.

Paige looked over at the boy. His face had soured with disgust.

"It's just a moth," she said. "Just a bug."

"It's dirty," he said.

"Not really," she murmured, conscious of the slight heat of the two filled pouches on her back. Another moth had found her just last night and deposited its eggs in one of the empty chambers. There were still two vacancies.

"My dad hates them," Evan said, still staring at the moth. "He wants to kill them all with bugspray." Evan looked back at the magazine on his lap. He seemed, suddenly, to become aware that he had no interest in its contents. He shut it, putting it on the coffee table to his left, and began hunting around for something else to read.

"Does your dad feel that way about all kinds of bugs?" Paige asked. Evan shrugged but did not answer. "Well," Paige said, if only to keep the conversation going. "I think they're pretty." It was an incomplete truth, but true nonetheless. "And they're an important part of the ecosystem."

Evan looked at Paige with a blank expression.

"You know what an ecosystem is?" she asked.

"Yeah," Evan said, insulted.

"So you know that without tenant moths, the bats might go hungry."

"Bats are dirty, too."

"Well, what about the flowers that the moths pollinate? You don't want the flowers to die, do you?"

"I didn't say I wanted it. I said my dad does." Evan gave up on the magazines and slouched back in his chair, eyes wide, lips pressed together.

Paige swallowed back all the arguments rising in her throat, realizing that she had walked into dangerous territory with the boy.

"Hey, Pumpkin Pie." It was Taja. She crouched in front of Evan, her hands on either armrest of his chair.

"Hi," Evan said.

"You doing okay?"

Evan didn't answer Taja's question.

"You want to play a game?"

Evan gave such a small nod that it was almost imperceptible.

"Okay, I've got Monopoly, Sorry, checkers, Hippos. I'm not sure what else. Let's go look." Taja stood up and offered Evan her hand. He took it. "Thanks so much, hon," Taja said to Paige and headed over with Evan to the shelves of games by the reception desk.

Paige sat in her chair feeling pointless and clumsy. She fought back waves of embarrassment as she rehearsed all that she had done wrong today: gasping at Mandy's face, forgetting to bring her lunch, forcing Evan to talk about his dad in the immediate aftermath of his trauma. This was the point of education, she reminded herself, to learn how to become less pointless, less clumsy. But she couldn't forgive herself just yet. The question of saving was not even on the table.

Paige watched the moth crawling patiently around the screen, its antennae in constant motion as it walked back and forth, looking for an opening.

"Just make sure there are no gaps," Paige said, handing a roll of medical tape to her sister.

"Are you sure about this?" Heather asked, her sculpted eyebrows pinched together prettily.

"Yes, I'm sure," Paige answered. They had plans to go out, but Paige had pulled her sister into the bathroom, tape in hand, and asked her—feigning casualness—to tape closed the two unoccupied chambers on her back.

"Is it even allowed?"

"What do you mean, 'Is it allowed?' Who do you think is in charge here? There aren't laws."

"Huh."

"Did you really think there were laws forcing me to host tenant moths?"

"I never thought about it."

That, Paige knew, was true. After that first night, Heather hadn't touched Paige's back again. Eventually, she even stopped eavesdropping on the lectures on tenancy and family history. Paige would be trapped there, listening as their mother unburdened herself of all the things she could tell no one else.

"Does Mom know you're doing this?" Heather asked. She peeled the medical tape from the roll, tearing off inch-long pieces and sticking them on her finger in a line.

"No." Paige was annoyed at the question, and she turned her back to her sister, both to avoid her eyes and to present the chambers for the tape. The scoop back of her billowy top made for easy access.

"Don't you think you should tell her?" Heather set the roll of tape on the bathroom counter.

"Why?"

"Don't be stupid."

"I'm not. I just don't think it's any of her business."

"Whatever," Heather said, and she began taping the chamber openings shut. "Just these two, right?" she asked. Paige looked back to see Heather pointing to the catty-corner empty chambers in the mirror. The occupied chambers were now reddened and a little puffy.

"Yeah," Paige said. "Just the empty ones." She felt sure Heather was avoiding touching the chambers with her bare fingers as she taped.

Paige turned her eyes to the bathroom window, a dark square of night framed into the wall. Even now, there was probably at least one moth pacing on her window frame, anxious to get to her. It made her uncomfortable, to be perceived with such intensity.

"All done," Heather said.

When Paige turned around, Heather plunked the roll of tape into her palm.

"Ready?" she asked Paige, putting on a carefree smile. "I can drive."

At the bar, Heather asked whether Paige could drink.

"Yeah," Paige said, raising her voice over the music, "it's fine. I probably shouldn't go crazy, but it's okay."

"Cool," Heather said and ordered their first round.

"It's hot in here," Paige said. "Do you have a hair tie?" Heather took one out of her purse and handed it to her sister. Paige swept her hair up into a ponytail, relieved to have it off her neck.

Heather lifted their sidecars off the bar and nodded towards an empty booth. "Let's sit." They slid in over the curved, padded bench until they met in the middle.

"I'm so over this scene," Heather said, taking a sip of her cloudy-orange drink. "Men do not leave me alone at these places. You'd think that I could at least have some good conversations, but let me tell you, they do not care what's going on in here." She tapped her head.

"Yeah, I bet." Paige fiddled with the curl of orange peel on the edge of her glass.

"Trust me, Paigelina. Being this cute has its drawbacks." She made a goofy face, trying—though not too hard—to mock her own beauty. "There's really nothing to be jealous of."

"I'm not jealous of you, Heather."

"I know, that's what I'm saying. Uh-oh. See what I'm talking about?" Heather pointed. A tall, scruffy-faced man was approaching their booth. Heather took a big drink of her sidecar and smiled up at him.

"Hi," he said. He looked to be in his late twenties, maybe a boyish thirty-something. He was loose and easy in his walk and seemed to hang together by suggestion alone.

"Hi," Heather said, her voice playful but aggressive. "Can we help you?"

"I'm Greg." He had a lopsided smile.

Heather propped her fingers together in front of her. "Whatcha want, Greg?"

"Just looking for someone to talk to."

Paige snorted. "Sorry, Heather was *just* telling me how men don't like to talk to her. So…." She gave a hokey shrug.

"Then I'll talk to you," Greg said and plunked down on Paige's end of the booth, a wide curve of cushion between them. She caught the scent of cloves.

"Oh, okay," Paige laughed. She turned to Heather, who raised her eyebrows in surprise over the rim of her drink. Paige looked back to Greg. "What do you want to talk about?"

Greg leaned back and cocked his head to think. "Please don't tell me what you do for work. I want something real." He leaned forward again. "When's the last time you had a flat tire?"

Paige thought about it. "Never."

Greg grinned. "Wow. Never?"

"Seriously, never?!" Heather echoed, swirling the remainder of her drink with more flair than was strictly necessary, but Greg was still looking at Paige. Paige wondered how long Heather's good mood would last if Greg never turned that easy-going smile on her.

"Nope," Paige said, looking from Heather back to Greg.

"Not even, like, on a bicycle?"

"Nope."

Greg crossed his arms and beamed at Paige. "Wow, you're good luck. I've always said that about keepers."

Paige straightened and pinched the stem of her glass uncomfortably.

Heather dropped her jaw. "Woah, how did you know?"

"I'm sorry," Greg said to Paige, scratching his half-grown beard nervously. "I noticed when you put your hair up. I don't mean to be a creep. I know a lot of people are weird about it, but I think it's awesome."

"Are you one, too?" Heather asked stiffly. At the bar, a triad of middle-aged men let out a howl of groans and oohs in response to some unheard jibe.

Greg shook his head. "I wish."

"You do?" Heather blurted. She looked sideways at Paige but didn't stop herself. She had always been a light touch with alcohol, and she had finished her drink quickly. "You *want* that?" She shuddered. "No offense," she said to Paige, "but it's not like *you* even want it, and you have it."

"You don't?" Greg asked, giving Paige a pained look. "Is that what the tape is all about?"

Paige didn't know what to say. She glared at her sister.

Heather rolled her eyes. "You're the one who made me tape your damn holes up!" She tipped her glass to get the last drops.

"I'm not exactly sure what I want." Paige ran her thumb through the wet of her glass and rubbed it between her fingers.

"Why not?" Greg insisted. "What happens between you and the moths—it's beautiful. It's a miracle. Excuse me for geeking out, but did you know that tenant moths are keystone pollinators for Hesperides' Trumpet? And *that's* what they use to make Clozanagen, which is a treatment for lymphoma."

Paige pushed at her drink as Greg spoke. "No, I know that," she said.

"And it's like, who else gets to do this? Be part of the life cycle of another species. Multiple other species when you think about it. You have this whole biome that you anchor. None of the rest of us have that. Nothing in this world is better off with us here. You're so lucky."

Paige shrugged uncomfortably. She could feel the eggs inside their chambers. That was impossible, though. They were so small. In her. Not her. Her tenants.

"Okay, I'm out," Heather said, forcing a laugh. "You two have fun. I'm going to go dance."

Paige watched her sister prance into the room, saw the half-dozen faces that turned towards her, as if it were compulsory. When she looked back at Greg, she found his eyes still on her. Their expression was tender.

"I dated this woman for a few years, a while back," he said, his eyes drifting from Paige's face to the caddy of condiments. "She was amazing. She would start the season down south, wherever the first reports came out. She would go outside at night totally naked, totally open. She had all her tenants within, like, two days of the first emergence. She'd hang out until her chambers were clear, then she'd drive up to wherever the emergence was at that point and do it again. She could do, like, three or four tenancies a year. I used to go with her, and it was so beautiful, like we were part of something, you know?"

"I don't know," Paige said.

"What is there not to know?" Greg's eyes were firmly on Paige again. He was wearing that lopsided grin. "It's like, you have your life's purpose told to you. Everyone else, they have to muddle around and figure that out without any clues. But you? It's different. It's like the universe is talking directly to you." He winced. "Look, you have to block out all that crap that people say. Keepers aren't..." He leaned towards Paige, his tone desperately earnest. "...there's nothing wrong with you."

Paige's lips tightened. "I know there's nothing wrong with me."

"What I mean is, it's the opposite. There's something *right* about you. You—people like you—it's the next level of humanity. It's evolution. It's everything." Greg shook his head, seemingly overwhelmed by the truth of what he had just spoken. "Please," he said, extending one hand towards Paige's on the table, taking her hand, holding it. His palm was as tough and smooth as a leather jacket. Part of her could think of nothing except his hand. Part of her itched to pull her hand away. "Please. Promise me one thing."

"Promise you?"

"Promise me you won't get the surgery."

Paige pulled her hand into her lap. "Dude. You don't even know my name."

"But I know *you*," he said, tears rising in his eyes.

"You really don't. Excuse me." Paige scooted out of the booth and went to find Heather.

"Can we go?" she shouted over the music, leaning towards her sister's ear.

"Really?" Heather made a pouty face. "He was cute, though."

"Please?"

"Okay, whatever." Heather went to the bar to settle up and then edged her way to the door, Paige following in her wake.

Outside, walking the two blocks to Heather's car, Heather kept looking over at Paige and shaking her head.

"What?" Paige asked, finally.

"Nothing." But then Heather stopped, in front of the rolled-down grille of a storefront café. "I just—I don't know what you want."

Paige tensed. "Are you talking about the chambers?"

"Yes, that. And the guy. You complain all the time how people are so grossed out by keepers. Well, he wasn't grossed out. And he was *cute*."

"I don't complain all the time. And he was a creep. He was *too* interested."

"You're ridiculous. You get so much attention for those stupid moth sacs. But now it's like, No thank you, tape 'em up! What do you want, Paige?"

"What do you mean, what do I want? I just want to be a person."

"Then be a person. No one is stopping you."

"You don't get it, Heather. I *can't*. Even when they're empty, they're waiting. It's like I'm more than a person or less than one—I don't know. Maybe I don't know what I want. More time? What I really want is to have my life back, but this time I want it without them. But I can't have that. So I taped them up. It's not what I want, but it's something."

Heather turned toward the lowered grille and linked her fingers through its bars. She peered at the glass of the entryway. "It's not like it's easy *not* having them," she said to Paige's reflection.

Paige stared back into the window, but Heather's face was obscured by shadow. "You want mine?" she asked. Heather gave a stiff laugh, a rush of air with no voice in it. Behind them, a car passed with its music playing loud, thumping into their chests.

Heather turned away from the café and wiped her eyes. "You're impossible. You know that? Just impossible." She took Paige's arm, and they walked on towards the car.

After Heather dropped her off, Paige stood in her bathroom, paused in the middle of her nighttime routine, the toothbrush clenched between her teeth. She kept thinking about her conversation with Heather. What could be easier than not having the chambers? Heather had flaunted the ease of not having them all their lives. She had built walls between herself and Paige and defended them. She didn't want to know anything, hear anything, see anything that might complicate matters.

Just then, Paige's phone, face down on the window ledge by the toilet, rang. Paige turned the phone over to see who it was.

"Tattletale," Paige said, her mouth full of toothpaste foam. She spat into the sink, did a quick rinse, and answered. "Hi, Mom."

"What are you doing, Paige?"

Paige knew what her mom was asking, but she didn't feel like being cooperative. She wandered out of the bathroom, past the bed, and into the dark of the living room. "Nothing. I'm just getting ready for bed. What's up?"

"Heather told me what you asked her to do."

"Mom…." Paige flopped herself onto the couch, staring up at the fanned pattern of the apartment's plaster ceiling. The light from the bedroom door was long and stark across its surface.

"Paige, you have to take the tape off."

"No, I don't."

"If they can't get to you, they can't deposit."

"I have two tenants already, Ma."

"That's what Heather said…." Paige could hear her mother sigh in that way she had, almost a whimper. "Why didn't you tell me when it happened?"

"I didn't know you wanted to know," Paige said, rubbing her eyes, reminding herself of Irina with this gesture of weariness.

"Of course I want to know! It's your first time. I thought you would tell me."

"Well, I'm sorry. But you know now, so… whoop-de-doo. I have moths."

"You have two open, though. I bet if you went outside right now, you could get both deposits tonight. It's a very active time."

Paige imagined this: picking the tape off and standing under the parking lot lights in her pajamas. Her back crawling with green-and-grey moths with dark-splotched wings, their velvet abdomens slipping eggs into the chambers of her back. It wasn't a fearful thought to her. But it wasn't fear that had made her ask Heather to tape her up. It wasn't fear that led her to lock her windows as soon as she got home, that kept her here inside. It was something just as urgent but less fleeting.

"No, Mom. I'm not going outside. I don't want the other chambers filled. I wish I had taped them all up before it was too late."

"Paige!"

"What? Mom! I don't want them. I'm allowed to decide that."

"Who told you that?"

"No one told me. It's just how it is."

There was no answer to this, at first. Paige checked the phone to make sure they were still connected. When her mother spoke again, she sounded strange—it was a tone Paige had never heard her use before. It was not cajoling, not scolding, not flattering or soothing. Her voice was bare, somehow. It embarrassed her to hear her mother sound like this.

"You kids think your lives are all about you. They're not."

Paige was taken aback. "All about me? That's not fair, Mom. I do plenty of things for other people. But my body *is* about me."

"No, it's not." Paige half-laughed at such an audacious statement, but her mother kept going: "You are part of something, Paige. Your body is part of it. God designed you in a very specific way for a very specific purpose. You don't get to opt out of his plan for you. You don't get to choose who you are."

"Mom!"

"I'm serious. I'm sick of all this nonsense about, 'You can be whatever you want to be.' I never told you girls that. You have gifts and you have obligations, and you are responsible to both of those things."

"But Mom, if I don't want it, it's not a gift. It's clutter." Paige kicked herself for saying this and sat up on the couch, ready for a fight, but her mother wasn't saying anything. "Mom, I'm sorry. I know it's not like that for you, but... I'm not you. That has to be okay."

"It's not okay, Paige. It's not. You have a responsibility. Now, do it." And she hung up.

Paige leaned back on the couch, looking up at the half-lit ceiling.

Someone had made those fan shapes in the plaster. There had been a person on a ladder, she thought, their ridged trowel moving in gentle arcs, one after another. Had this worker, this artist, imagined her, some future occupant of the apartment, sitting in this room staring at the ceiling? Perhaps the fan shapes were there for their own sake. Because the ceiling was a blank asking to be filled with some sort of intention. Paige put herself on that ladder, smoothing the ceiling back out, returning it to emptiness.

God's design, her mother had said. His plan for her. But if God were real—the God her mother believed in, the God who created all things and held the vast universe in mind at all times—then God was too powerful a being to understand the implication of its choices in a human life. What did such a being know of vulnerability, of anxiety, of longing for erasure? But Paige didn't think that God was real. She didn't believe in whatever Greg was peddling, either: that the universe, speaking the language of evolution and interconnectedness and whatever else, had determined her purpose and written it into her back.

Was it worse, that there was no plan for her? It was the same loneliness and powerlessness, in the end, to think that one was misjudged and misperceived and to know that one was not perceived at all but merely circumstantial. Those warm pockets between her shoulder blades were filled with someone else's life—a life that was no part of her. It was another being's need and ambition that sought her out, desired her. Like Heather: pursued, everyone thinking about her, trying to get close to her, but she herself was irrelevant. Paige felt herself the object of all this attention—her mother's, Greg's, God's, the moths'—but she herself was see-through, a screen in the shape of a person. Being a keeper—it was so little a thing. Too little. It threatened to shrink her away to nothing.

And Paige wanted to be something. Beyond her hot, dark little chambers, the world was large with importance. There was Evan. His father, blood on his hands, teaching his son what was dirty and deserving of violence. His mother, faced with the impossible question of what she needed. When Paige went back in the morning, Mandy and Evan wouldn't be there. They would be staying in a room in the shelter across town, or else they would have gone back home—persisting day after day. Their lives—so broad and unknowable—had met with Paige's in a fleeting touch and then pulled away. In this exchange, she had been the parasite—timid and fragile, slow and peripheral, using their pain to learn her profession.

What would it take to truly face up to such enormity? How did Irina do it? By filling out all those papers? How did Taja? By eating salad at her desk and playing games with sad boys? These women could teach her about their work—the concessions to bureaucracy required to step towards justice. But perhaps Paige, bound to the little things inside of her, was already too small to meet the world in its entirety.

So what, then? Should she quit the program? She could get some other job—any other job—that began and ended and did not crawl inside of her and reside there. She could add columns or rack up sales or something. She could untape her back and accept that which came to her on green-edged wings, soft and assuming.

Paige stood up from the couch and went to the window that looked down onto the parking lot. In the orange lights, a swarm of insects flashed and fluttered. Heather was right. To go outside and let the moths intersect their little lives with hers—that would be the easy thing, like signing a form, checking a box. She wouldn't have to do anything—just sit there and let the soft-footed moth crawl across her back. The harder choice was emptiness. Paige turned and walked into the bright bedroom. She switched off the light in the bathroom, the tall lamp by the dresser. Curled in bed, she set her alarm and placed her phone on the bedside table, its charger cord snaking down to the outlet. Then she flipped over onto her stomach. In her back, pale green larvae were growing tight in their eggs; perhaps the first were already beginning to hatch.

Let them hatch, then. Let them work their way out of her body and leave her vacant. She would not let them fill her up again. It was time to stop signing her name to contracts that she had not read. She took a breath so deep it burned her lungs. When she let it out, there was relief in it. Resolve. Never again. She would safeguard the space within her. She would close herself off. She would remain undetermined, uncluttered by anyone's gifts.

M. C. Benner Dixon lives, writes, and grows things in Pittsburgh, PA. She is quick to make a pun and slow to cut her grass. Her short stories have appeared in *Funicular*, *The Los Angeles Review*, *The Hopper*, *Fusion Fragment*, and elsewhere. Christine's writing includes a collection of craft essays, co-authored with Sharon Fagan McDermott, forthcoming from the University of Michigan Press. Her debut novel, *The Height of Land*, is the recipient of the 2022 Orison Fiction Prize. Christine is the Adult Program Director for Write Pittsburgh. Find her on Twitter @mchristinebd or at bennerdixon.com.

Exception

Marissa Lingen

Surely I will breathe fresh air
Surely I will drink clean water
Surely I will not suffer alone
Surely I will not rage with fever
Surely I will not be turned away
To cramp and bleed unaided
Surely I will root in rich1 soil
Surely my voice will be heard
For what I meant, not what I said;
For what I should have meant.
Surely my trees will not burn,
Nor my bridges, nor my books.
Surely I am not one of *those* people
Surely I have nothing to fear
Surely I will never lie down
In this bed someone else has made,
A stranger in the land I thought I knew.

Marissa Lingen is a freelance writer living in the suburbs of Minneapolis with her family. Mostly she writes speculative fiction. She has a large collection of foliage-themed jewelry.

www.ingramcontent.com/pod-product-compliance
Lightning Source LLC
Chambersburg PA
CBHW061456210726
48287CB00007B/2538

* 9 7 8 1 9 5 5 3 6 0 0 7 4 *